THE ART OF SPIRITUAL WRITING

'There's a lovely phrase at the start of the Anglo-Saxon epic when Beowulf the hero says he is going to "unlock his word-hoard", meaning the treasury of language that will express the essence of his story. You are on a journey of your own, no less epic, to discover and explore the treasure within you. Eirene Palmer and Richard Palmer's *The Art of Spiritual Writing* offers a delightfully accessible, practical and comprehensive guide to making this journey through writing, beginning with the single step of picking up a pen or opening a laptop. It presents a whole range of different approaches – an invaluable set of keys to help you unlock your own "word-hoard" and let your soul tell her story.'

**Margaret Silf,
author of *Landmarks, Wayfaring,
Hidden Wings* and *Born to Fly***

THE ART OF SPIRITUAL WRITING

*Discovering your most
authentic writing ... and
more about yourself
on the way*

EIRENE PALMER &
RICHARD PALMER

DARTON·LONGMAN+TODD
INTELLIGENT ♦ INSPIRATIONAL ♦ INCLUSIVE
SPIRITUAL BOOKS

First published in 2025 by
Darton, Longman and Todd Ltd
Unit 1, The Exchange
6 Scarbrook Road
Croydon CR0 1UH

editorial@darton-longman-todd.co.uk

This product conforms to the requirements of the European Union's
General Product Safety Regulations (GPSR).

EU Authorised Representative for GPSR:
Easy Access System Europe –
Mustamäe tee 50, 10621 Tallinn, Estonia
gpsr.requests@easproject.com

© 2025 Richard and Eirene Palmer

The right of Richard and Eirene Palmer to be identified as the
Authors of this work has been asserted in accordance with the
Copyright, Designs and Patents Act 1988.

ISBN: 978-1-915412-92-8

A catalogue record for this book is available from the British Library.

Designed and produced by Judy Linard

Printed and bound in Great Britain by Short Run Press, Exeter

For our children George, Tom, Sarah,
Tim, Jack and Lucy.
And to all those who have helped us
on our own spiritual and writing journeys,
far too many to mention.

But from me, Eirene, for Chrissie,
my priest-friend – for helping me
discover who I am.

And for me, Richard, to the memory of
Aunty Betty and Uncle Steve, early enablers
and encouragers who opened my eyes
to new horizons.

Contents

Authors' note	9
Introduction	11
Chapter 1: Where to begin	15
Chapter 2: My past journey	28
Chapter 3: Present times	51
Chapter 4: Looking forward	73
Chapter 5: Freewriting	90
Chapter 6: Spiritual Journalling	102
Chapter 7: Writing as therapy	117
Chapter 8: Writing as prayer	131
Chapter 9: The marvellous metaphor	149
Chapter 10: And finally …	164
Chapter 11: Signposts	168

Authors' note

There have been many pleasures and treasures in the writing of this book, the pleasures of the writing itself and the unexpected treasures that all writing reveals. And, of course, there have been the sticky and the tricky bits, where you go back again and take another run at it.

Before we set out to put pen to paper, we thought co-authoring a book might prove a bit complex and messy. The reality was quite the opposite. Together, we had already developed and delivered a lot of the material for this book over a number of years through many retreats, courses, seminars, talks and articles. Working together on all of those ventures meant our views on the contents of the book were fully aligned. Add to that the ongoing cross-editing we did on each other's work, the resulting tweaking, massaging, margin-scribbles and coffee-time discussions, we discovered we could write the book by using the pronoun 'WE' to tell our story. In fact, when we read through our final manuscript, we had difficulty in several places deciding who had written certain parts.

Nevertheless, we are conscious that at times when one of us has a personal story to tell, we will need to revert to the pronoun 'I'. In those circumstances, we annotate the text to tell you who is the storyteller. I (Eirene), or I (Richard). And in some chapters, where one of us has more expertise and interest in a topic, we will spell out who is writing.

To give you a clear run to start, the *Introduction* is Eirene's, and *Chapter One* is Richard's. After that, things will

The Art of Spiritual Writing

become evident. The book is about the spiritual journey, or life's journey as we like to call it. So, consider the book as a journey as well. Don't be too concerned with who is talking. We are both present throughout the whole of this journey. And we hope you enjoy the trip and find lots to interest you along the way.

Introduction

Who am I? That's a question which has bugged us all from the moment we first became conscious that the world extended further than the end of the garden. Even if we weren't aware of it.

If you consider yourself a spiritual being inhabiting an earthly body (and that's just about all of us) – how do you explore your-self? And how do you make a connection with that part of you which drives you in your innermost being? That part of you which yearns for God – or whatever name you may use for the being who is quite literally our breath of life.

Some would call this process prayer. And it is. But there are a myriad ways to pray and it can be helpful to 'pray as you can, not as you can't.' We think that one of the most powerful ways is through words. Writing. Finding your voice. Discovering your authentic self through your most authentic writing.

And that is what this book is about. Writing about our spiritual lives and writing from that deep reflective place inside each of us. Our own journeys, past, present and future, mapping those areas of unique individual interest to us. Discovering the value of writing meditative and reflective work, the benefits of writing for therapy and prayer. Exploring good journalling practices and daily writing.

You can use this book in whatever way works best for you. Read it front to back in one sitting with a glass of red or a mug of hot chocolate. Read it on the beach, a page at a

The Art of Spiritual Writing

time sandwiched between retrieving the beach ball for the kids and hammering the pegs for the windbreak into the sand for the seventeenth time. Read it on the bus (though not if, like me, you are easily made travel sick). Read it in the bath, drop it and prise open the soggy pages to find where you were up to. Read it in bed and let it fall to the floor as you drift off ...

Read it as you can, not as you can't.

It's written – as most books are, with a beginning, a middle and an end and to be honest, it's best if you read the first chapter first. This is your map to tell you where you are going. Then you can either stick to the map and read it all the way through, or you can go off-road and read the chapters that interest you most. (I like doing that.) Find your own natural flow.

Because this book is all about that – finding yourself, finding your flow – finding your voice. And essential to this process of finding your voice is talking about finding connection. More specifically – connection to God.

I find God in writing. I find God in writing the things I didn't say and wished I had – to other people and to God. I write to fill the gaps – to make sense of the times when I felt hurt or ignored or abandoned. Like a lot of us I found it easier to push these things down deep where the sun doesn't shine than bring them out into the light. Because at the time, the light didn't feel very safe or accepting.

So this is an invitation to bring some of your-self into the light. As much as you want to. Find your voice and test it out in the clear light of day.

This book is written with the premise that everyone is spiritual. We run a community café in our local cathedral and our guests constantly confide that they don't go to church now but ... And that 'but' can encompass all the yearnings in our psyche, or soul if you like, for something bigger than ourselves. God. Love. Higher Power. And they light a candle, they sit in silence, they listen to the organist practising for Sunday, they are warmed and comforted.

Introduction

They have a coffee and a Tunnock's teacake and seem brighter. Maybe it's the Tunnock's teacake but most attest to some seeking and finding.

They seek a connection between themselves and someone or something else. Even if they can't name it.

So this book is written also for the seekers, the spiritual wanderers, the explorers, those in the borderlands. Those who want to set out on a spiritual coast-to-coast and need some tools for the walk. And those who maybe want to do just the first bit – say St Bees to Patterdale and see how they go.

You know how sometimes you see an advert for a cruise, or a boat trip, or a weekend away for two in the Cotswolds, and there's a picture of a happy, smiley couple clinking glasses and gazing deep into each other's eyes. They have white shiny teeth, shiny smiles, shiny hair, shiny skin and are set on a shiny background of palm trees/wooded forest/olde English tea shoppe and the message is, 'Come with us and you will experience this!' Connection. Happiness. One with another. Communion even.

Because that's what deep down, we all want because we are human. Even the most cantankerous, inhospitable, surly dude who has a big 'Keep Out' sign slung around his neck wants connection, deep inside. It's just a bugger to know how to ask for it sometimes.

You can ask for it in writing and it's one of the safest ways. Because you don't have to show it to anyone if you don't want to. But you'll have made a connection. With your-self. With God if you invite him/her to read it.

One of my very favourite quotes is attributed to Vine Deloria Jnr.: 'Religion is for those who are afraid of going to hell. Spirituality is for those who have already been there.' That means all of us. None of us is immune because we all have bits that go wrong, fall off, start hurting, break and wear out and the people we love will experience this too. So it follows that at some point, either we or those we love so dearly that we can't imagine the universe without them,

The Art of Spiritual Writing

will be either sick or not here. And that is very tough. And it's where spirituality is at its most active, most at work, as we call out to our Creator to help us out with this. It's not about ticking boxes on a score sheet which is what some religion can feel like some of the time. It's about connection.

So we invite you to chance connection. We invite you to pick up your pen, grasp your mouse, focus on your tablet or laptop or whatever works best for you and write. A few words. A work the size of *Ulysses*. Chance it. Try it. Write it.

Come journey with us!

CHAPTER 1

Where to begin

In a sense, this is what writing is like. You have all these ingredients, the details of your life, but just to list them is not enough. 'I was born in Brooklyn. I have a mother and a father. I am female.' You must add the heat and energy of your heart. This is not just any father; this is your father. The character who smoked cigars and put too much ketchup on his steak. The one you loved and hated … Nabokov says, 'Caress the divine details.'

Natalie Goldberg, *Writing Down the Bones*

Many years ago, I watched a TV interview with Marco Pierre White, the celebrity chef. He was asked about the occasion when he charged a customer £25 for a bowl of hand-cut chips in one of his restaurants. At that time this was an extortionate amount of money (still would be for a bowl of chips). In mitigation, he said something along the lines that chips were not on the menu, and he'd had to make them specially and hence it cost him a lot of time. Then he added something that has always stuck with me. He said that he thought they were cheap at the price because he was sure the person who bought them had been dining out on the story ever since.

I bet he was right, because it is a good story. And I'm confident to say that, because here I am telling it again. It is a personal event, a good story, with that fascinating *'Can you believe it?!'* element. No one else has this story. What is more,

The Art of Spiritual Writing

it comes from somewhere deep inside. And it has emotion in it. That initial outrage at the price, the disbelief. After the initial shock has subsided, you start to think that you must tell others about this. And perhaps you start to see the funny side.

As humans, we live off stories. They may be internal ones, playing through our minds, of something that happened yesterday, or what we are planning for the future. What's the story of your day going to look like? Stories are why we need to meet up for coffee or a chat to tell others our stories and importantly, to hear theirs. We exchange information through stories and get excited telling them to others. They are a huge part of our discourse in life and a substantial part of the human condition. What happened? Who was involved? We want to know the details and, of course, the outcome. Was it a happy ending?

Stories provide us with valuable imagery of what life is about. It is how we educate our children, telling them stories or reading them story books. Ever since our ancestors sat around the camp fire and shared information about surrounding dangers, the huge snake that has moved in by the lake, the good place to find fruit, stories have been key to our understanding of life and indeed to our safety and wellbeing. They leave a mark.

In fact, stories are almost as important as that bowl of chips we mentioned earlier. We need them. They nourish us as we tell them and they nourish us when we hear them. They are the bread of life. Without them, we feel an inner hunger. We need to tell you our stories, and we need to listen to yours. So please come round to see us for a chat.

And the best ones, the tales that we remember most, are those that come from the heart. They are powerful because they are unique and personal accounts of life, often emotional and with a deep personal meaning. That's what makes them resonate. They rock! And the story of the bowl of chips is a prime example.

So how does the idea of story fit in with the notion of spiritual writing?

Where to begin

What is spiritual writing?

Like all matters spiritual, it can be difficult to define. In essence, it is writing that comes from your heart and soul. Spiritual writing comes from a deep part of you. It is honest and authentic and often comes from a vulnerable place. It can be something that you have not revealed before, either to others or indeed to yourself. It is often insightful revelatory writing, something you didn't know you knew, something you didn't know you felt or believed, something that is only revealed to you as you articulate it on the page. Henri Nouwen talks of this in his book, *Bread for the Journey*, when he says, 'One of the most satisfying aspects of writing is that it can open in us deep wells of hidden treasures that are beautiful for us as well as for others to see.' You may also feel a spiritual movement, a godly connection, that '*bigger than me*' moment as you write, the eternal muse reaching out and touching you.

You can also view it another way and say that it is writing about spiritual matters. That tends by definition to include some of the previous descriptions. The bottom line is that it is writing from your spirit. And you'll feel it when you write it.

I certainly do. I'm a self-confessed blubberer. I used to be quite embarrassed about this until a spate of celebrities started to confess to it and it became quite competitive as to who could blub the most. I'm proud to say that I am almost at Olympic standard now and can even be moved by the Christmas TV ads. But at least I now know that I am not alone. My father passed on the gene to me and I've passed it down to a number of my children. So, when I reread a piece that I have written, and I well up moist-eyed, then I know that it is good and that it is spiritual writing and I know that others will tell me it is good. Please note, you don't have to be a blubberer to write. This is my own litmus test of moving writing. You will develop your own internal write-o-meter to measure your work.

We have used story here to illustrate spiritual writing,

but it is not just about story. Spiritual writing can be many things. Poetry or prose, a prayer or a reflection, letters, journal entries, articles, essays, any form of writing counts and they can all come from a spiritual depth. The use of story here is to help you to access sources from your past that can yield depth and lead to a greater recognition of your own spiritual writing.

Back to stories

Okay, many will accept that we all have these stories in our memory banks, but still feel inadequate with the idea of writing them down. Our proposition is that if you have the story, it is but a small step, a small step, note, to writing it down. It has never been easier to do this than now.

And with the writing down comes a power. You have recorded. And you can polish and hone your story until it shines. Now more people can hear it and suddenly you can discover one of the powers of writing. Your stories go a lot further, and when buffed up will be even better than their oral telling.

There's lots more to it of course but we want to help you to discover your authentic stories and how to write these down, how to search out and access those gems of fun or wisdom, hope, despair, love and longing. These will lead you to find your authentic writing voice and in so doing, you are likely to find out a lot more about yourself on the way.

I can best illustrate this with a short story about authentic writing. I belong to a small supervision group who meet every two months to share. It's a friendly group and we've been on a journey together for over nine years. After our meeting the other day, I contacted them by email with what grew unexpectedly into a little short story. But I wasn't sure whether to send it. Or not. It was a bit risqué in one part. But it made me laugh. I know, you shouldn't laugh at your own jokes but it had something about it. Hmm, should I? In

Where to begin

the end, I did send it and got an immediate response from the group saying how funny it was. 'I've just been reduced to a spluttering wreck with laughter – my hot drink sprayed all over the fruit bowl ... Brilliant, I love it. It's cheered up a gloomy afternoon' (thank you, Teresa!). I have to say that's some of the best direct immediate feedback I've had on my writing in a long time! But the point of this story is not that I'm bragging about my writing. It is solely that I was writing with my authentic voice. The telling of that little story represented the real me and because of that, it touched the small audience I sent it to in a very profound and humorous way. But note what I said about my hesitation in sending it. That was my internal censor getting in the way. We'll come back to that later in the book. And also note the very small group I sent it to. Again, we'll revisit that.

For now, let us assure you that you will read only our authentic writing voices in this book. There will be no stylised, contrived or affected material coming your way, but just the stuff we really believe in, the concepts and ideas that that we have gleaned in our extensive spiritual walks and our respective writing walks and that we feel are worthy of sharing.

But I can't write!

We hear this mantra so many times. Too many of us carry these messages throughout our life. And they are untrue testimonies that many end up believing, collected along the road from insecure or jealous folks around us, from an unhelpful comment of a teacher on your handwriting, from a problem with dyslexia, to being left-handed (my own personal experience). It can often be just one acerbic comment that has left its mark that can make you feel totally incompetent.

If you are reading this, you have learnt the basic principles of grammar, vocabulary, sentence structure and some spelling. If we have gone through school, we all have

The Art of Spiritual Writing

a basic understanding of these writing processes.

We hear of such discouragements regularly in our writing groups and retreats. Our response is always the same. You can all write. The likelihood is you have passed numerous exams, written countless essays, reports and assignments as a part of your education, sent innumerable letters and emails from work or personally, and maybe contribute on social media. You do write.

Roald Dahl writes in his interesting short story, 'Lucky Break: How I Became a Writer', of the awful reports he got in English Composition at his secondary school. He quotes several examples of his bad reports in this subject. One from Easter Term, 1931 (aged 15), reads: 'English Composition. "A persistent muddler. Vocabulary negligible, sentences malconstructed. He reminds me of a camel."' Don't be discouraged, it happens to the best of us! (Taken from *The Wonderful World of Henry Sugar and Six More*, Roald Dahl, Penguin 2017.)

What scares people from writing for their own enjoyment or benefit is the word '*writer*'! It immediately conjures up an image of a learned person at a large desk in their quiet study, surrounded by bookcases groaning with reference books, a studious frown upon their face as they tap out the most glorious golden prose on their keyboard, the completion of which is eagerly awaited by their publisher, who knows that their book will sell like hot cakes. Well, thank you Hollywood for that film script.

Here is the definition of a writer from the Concise Oxford English Dictionary 'Writer: a person who has written a particular text. A person who writes books or articles as a regular occupation.' Note that the first definition says, 'a person who has written a particular text'. Isn't that wonderful! Sadly, it's the second definition everyone hangs their hat on, that of the professional writer. We cannot stress this enough. You do not have to be a professional writer to call yourself a writer.

And there is also that other word that scares would-be

Where to begin

writers a lot – *book*. Writing does not mean that you will publish a book. We have been in writing groups where if you haven't published at least one or preferably two books, you really are not a writer. And that is rubbish. Repeat after me: 'You do not need to have published a book to call yourself a writer.'

We made the mistake when we first started our writing group of asking members at each of our meetings who had had any of their work published since we last met. Many in our group have got their writing published, but we soon realised this was not what the group was about. The group was here to encourage members of whatever level to write. We now ask what they are working on or what they have written, rather than what has been published.

Of course, many of us crave to be published. It is the icing on the cake. But it is just as valid to write something about your life to pass on to your children and grandchildren or to send an email or a letter to friends that will bring them joy.

To illustrate the point that all of us can write, reproduced below is a story my mother wrote way back in time in the mid-nineties. My daughter's primary school had asked the class of six-year-olds to bring their grandparents along to tell stories of their lives 'in the olden days.' Fortunately, my mother wrote the story down.

Washday in the 1930s, sent by Brenda Palmer, nanny to Lucy Palmer

When I was young and about eight years old, I began to realise that MONDAY was the big washing day, and went on until I got home from school about 4 pm. We had no hot water out a tap in those days. We had to boil a kettle or saucepans on a small gas cooker.

We lived in a small terraced cottage with two

downstairs rooms, with an open fire in each, had no bathroom, and we washed each morning in a bowl on the kitchen table. But we had a 'washhouse' across the yard, and to get to this, you had to walk across a small yard and up four steps. This is where all the washing was done. Also, once a week, we had a bath in there, in a metal bath measuring six feet long, which at other times hung on the wall.

The washhouse contained a large brick copper in the corner, a huge mangle with wooden rollers with a metal container underneath to catch the water. There was also a small sink with a cold water tap to rinse the clothes in and from which water was ladled into the copper.

There was a large metal tub, called a 'Dolly Tub' and 'Dolly Pegs' – a large wooden object operated by hand and swished from left to right continuously to get the clothes clean. There was also a metal board in the sink where the collars of the shirts and anything that needed extra scrubbing were rubbed with a bar of soap, up and down the board, to get them clean before transferring them to the copper. These types of boards are sometimes used by various Skiffle groups playing on the television.

The first job in the morning on Mondays was to light a fire under the copper to heat the water up ready to ladle into the dolly tub for the first colour wash. Then, before you started this wash, you had to fill the copper again ready for boiling the white cotton sheets. This wash also included my father's white coat and apron. As he worked in a grocer's shop, they had to be starched in Robin's Starch to make them nice and crisp. My mother also did her own mother's washing, as she was ill, and washed all the towels from a local hairdressers for

Where to begin

> the week for the sum of twelve and a half pence (two shillings and sixpence). I had to collect and return these.
>
> After boiling the sheets, these were lifted out with a very large wooden stick into a metal container, then through the mangle to get rid of a lot of the soapy water, then transferred to the sink to be rinsed in cold water and Reckitt's Blue, a small blue tablet used in the final rinse to give extra whiteness. (There used to be a huge advert saying 'Out of the Blue Comes the Whitest Wash'). Afterwards, all the sheets had to be mangled yet again, ready to hang on the line, weather permitting.
>
> When I got home for my lunch on Mondays, I invariably had to run half a mile to the grocer's shop and back to get something to eat, have my lunch and then run back to school, all within the hour, so I really remember 'MONDAY WASHDAY'.

I use this as an example for a number of reasons. My mother left school at fifteen. She became a typist and learnt typing and some shorthand but I never saw her read a book. Other than some old encyclopaedias, there were no adult books in our house. There was a daily red top and a *Woman's Weekly* magazine would appear from time to time. Ours was not a literary household. In other words, she was not a writer by any stretch and had a limited education. And yet, she produced this quite detailed and historically interesting story. I have not edited it. I rest my case that we can all write.

Secondly, the level of detail is quite striking. There is a real sense of the washhouse, its Edwardian laundry paraphernalia, up four steps, Reckitt's Blue and more. It was clearly a scenario she had witnessed repeatedly as a small child and the drudgery and hard work involved

The Art of Spiritual Writing

that took over the whole household every Monday had left its mark on her. It is a story that comes from a deep place, something not to be forgotten but to be shared with others. There would have been a joy for her to do this for her granddaughter, to read it out to the class and watch those cherubic faces listening to her story. It came from her heart and her soul. That's what makes it so captivating. It was her authentic voice. It was spiritual writing.

Thirdly, such writing produces a wonderful record of someone's life. When my mother died in 2014, we asked friends and family to send in a memory of her. These varied in length, from two pages long, a half a page, a couple of lines. We got 75 in total and included the three stories that she had written for the infant school as our respective children proceeded through its doors. The further two were entitled 'Summer holidays' and 'My schooldays'. Fortunately, I had kept these in a folder of my earlier writings and it was just a case of copy typing them into the word processor. We circulated this written collection of memories to all who contributed material. And so, they live on, a record of a person's life.

The idea of collecting such stories when someone close to you dies is a golden idea that we recommend. The whole exercise of this book of remembrance was very much about spiritual writing. It was not only a deeply spiritual occasion, marking someone's death. All the contributors trawled their minds for the memorable, poignant, loving and often humorous stories of her life. In other words, they looked for the stories from deep within. Spiritual writing.

Fourthly, you never know where your writing will go to. When my mother wrote the Washday story, it was for a class of six-year-olds. It has gone into her book of remembrance. And she would not have believed in her wildest dreams that it would now be appearing in a book. Never underestimate the power of story, nor to where it will travel and who will read it.

Finally, this example is about telling stories. My mother was good at telling stories. I have fondest memories of

Where to begin

Christmas Eve parties when both sets of grandparents visited. After the sherry bottle was uncorked, or as we got more sophisticated, the Advocaat Snowballs appeared, complete with a glacé cherry on a stick, mind (I can still smell them) and a couple of light ales were uncapped for the men, the stories would start. I began to realise that the telling of one story would lead on automatically to another. For instance, we'd hear the tale of my grandfather, Fred, having the engine from the motorbike and sidecar still in bits on the kitchen floor the Friday night before they were to set off early the following morning for their week's camping holiday in Skegness. This would lead on to the story of my other grandfather, George, a grocer's assistant, who was used to delivering the groceries to the villages by horse and cart. In time, he was promoted to take the deliveries out in the new delivery van. (This was in the 1950s - interesting to note how today's supermarkets think they've invented something special with their home deliveries!) Not being a driver, he drove all the way home from a distant village with the handbrake on and burnt out the brakes. And so on, to much laughter and merriment as more family legends were aired and another round of Snowballs was produced as cheese and pineapple on sticks, sausage rolls and dishes of salted peanuts were handed round.

Even if you don't consider yourself a consummate story teller, you will have a catalogue of stories that you bring out in conversation with others. They may be historical or very recent, what you heard on the bus today, something you caught on the radio. We are all story tellers, or as we like to say, *storysmiths*, because we have all lived a conscious life. Such stories are the gems that will help you to develop your authentic writing voice. They are dear to your heart. Write them down for others to enjoy and benefit from. Imagine the story and put it into words. That's all you have to do. Write it down as it occurs to you. Write them down to discover more about yourself, and write them down to experience the joy of writing.

Still to come ...

'Fear not, said he, for mighty dread had seized their troubled mind', as Nahum Tate wrote way back in the late 1600s, when he composed his famous carol, 'While shepherds watched their flocks by night'. If you have not written stories down before, you may feel hesitant to have a go at doing it. Relax with the idea. There is lots of easy help coming your way and we've broken things down into easy bites.

Remember that it has never been easier to transfer your thoughts into writing. It is so easy to get the written word onto the page with modern digital devices. A lot of us have grown to become consummate or passable typists. But there are other means. The ability to dictate your work into such devices is commonly available. If this helps you to start with, do just that. Tell the story to your device. Then you have your first draft. It will need further work embellishing, polishing and editing, because the spoken word can be sketchier than the written word. But you've taken the first step and put your first draft onto paper.

We'll show you how to identify key elements and their associated stories from your past. We will give you lots of leads and ideas to follow to help you to access those stories. There are prompts to help you to consider your present situation and moving forward, there are tips on writing about the future. There are sections on the power of journalling, how to make the most of your journal and how to develop your own particular style. We'll look at metaphors and parables as a way of exploring and expressing your thinking. We will show how to free up your writing and find a freedom to say what is on your mind. And we'll look at writing for therapy and writing as prayer. And to finish, if you wish to go further, there are lots of ideas about moving on beyond this book and growing in your authentic voice.

And on the way, there are short tips and writing prompts for you to try in each chapter. These are not compulsory. You are not at school and there's no one looking over your shoulder. so be creative, experiment and

Where to begin

be happy to make mistakes. The only advice we'd give you is to write from your heart, be honest and enjoy the process of getting it down on paper. Our hope is that you will grow in your writing confidence and that you will find here fresh ideas, suggestions and new insights to encourage you on your way.

Dip in and out of what speaks to you at this point. Don't be afraid to highlight, underline, scribble notes in the margins. Use this as a resource of ideas. It won't all appeal to you, but hopefully, many parts of it will. An important note is to say that there is no right or wrong way of doing what we cover here. It's up to you how you use the information and ideas. Enjoy it and suck the juice out of the tastiest bits. That's a metaphor!

From storysmith to wordsmith. It's not difficult. Honest. We shall explore lots of ways to do this as we share some of our spiritual journeys aka our life journeys and bring this together with our writing journeys to help you cross that bridge.

Writing prompts

Write as you can, not as you can't

Imagine one of your favourite stories that you tell to others. Or it can be a situation that you related to someone else over the past few weeks. Write it down quickly in under 500 words. A couple of hundred words will do. It is likely to be very rough around the edges or just odd notes. No matter. Put it to one side and leave it for two weeks. We'll come back to it.

CHAPTER 2

My past journey

Anybody who has survived his childhood has enough information about life to last him the rest of his days.
Flannery O'Connor, *Mystery and Manners,*
Occasional prose

The past. This is your most abundant source of stories, a Pandora's Box of ideas. Our minds are continually hopping around thinking about today and tomorrow. The beauty of the past as a good hunting ground for personal stories is that the stories are mainly complete. Their effects may have lasted but the events have been, gone, and are completed. This chapter contains many ideas and sources from which to recover the gems that you'd like to write about.

We are so fortunate to be here. For most of us it all started one day when two folks, aka our parents, got together, made love (take a moment, we know it's a difficult one) and shebang, nine months or so later out we popped, blinked, cried, took a look around, quite liked the look of what we saw and settled down to get on with living and growing. It's something that we take as natural. So what's the big deal?

My past journey

Well, the big deal is that we are here, real conscious beings who can talk, walk, work, love, sleep, read, write, go to the supermarket and generally try to do our bit to keep the world turning. Each of us is a totally unique creation, a never-to-be-repeated offer to humanity. Amazing! But what is even more amazing is how we take it all for granted.

Unlike the baby turtle, we don't come fully equipped. These little critters hatch out of their eggs, leg it across a treacherous beach as if their lives depended on it, which of course they do. And if they make it to the water's edge, they dive in and swim for their dear lives to find a safe refuge where they can take stock and start living their best lives.

Ours is a different experience of gradual development and slow maturing. And during this period, there is much that shapes our character and personality. For starters, our DNA sets out a few immoveable cornerstones. Then other major influences start to dictate the shape of things to come. Our ethnicity and gender, country of birth, our education and religion, our relationships and family to name but a few. These are critical. Add to these the many life events that come our way to cheer us on our way or stop us in our tracks and our true self begins to fill out as we become a complex human being.

When we come to try and think about who we are and what we might choose to write about ourselves, it can be tricky. If only our minds were like a piece of well-ordered software containing neatly-filed folders, from which we could access the specific information we require. Our minds are more often a swirling mess. It's like a great big tureen of soup. Stir it round and all sorts of items float to the top, ingredients that you had forgotten about, tasty morsels that sink again out of sight. How do we start to capture some of these ingredients, fish them out and ladle them into a bowl so that we can see what we have and turn it into a story? Many of us want to do just this, record something of our lives, explore who we are, look at what we've done and where we'd like to go next. And many simply echo what someone said recently as her self-introduction on one our retreats, 'I just want to write something down for my kids.'

Capturing the past

How do we start? Some people set out to write their story by thinking in slots of five or ten years and amass a lot of detail. There's nothing wrong with this but it can turn into a rather bland diary. Does it matter the exact date you got promoted to section leader at work or bought the new sofa? Such a detailed diary of information can be useful if the police come knocking on your door and ask you where you were on March 21st 2018 at 6 p.m. and you are able to tell them that you had sausage and mash for tea at 6 p.m. as usual, watched *The One Show*, *EastEnders* and the *Skyfall* repeat and went to bed at 10.30 p.m. But what we all want to hear is the colour of your life, the shouts of joy, the tumbles and the grit, the hills and hollows of your walk, your thoughts, the love and laughter, tears and sorrows. It's all there if you take a look into that rich tureen of soup.

The big idea that we like tremendously is to start with a small detail. We talk about putting the situation under the microscope and alighting on a small detail. Many writers use this. Anne Lamott in her book, *Bird by Bird* talks specifically about a one-inch picture frame that she has on her desk, a reminder to start with something small. We find this idea of starting small so often leads you into some rich, fertile and unexpected places.

> A personal example from me. I (Richard) have an old 1950s tandem in the family that was acquired in my teen years. One of my sons was moving home and had been the custodian of this very old machine for many years but no longer had the space to store it. The rest of the kids were lukewarm to the idea of taking it on and asked on its origin. I said I'd jot down a few

> notes as I hoped someone would take it on and save it from eBay.
>
> My intention was to write 500 words on where it came from. But as I started to write, I realised this item had a thread that ran through a good part of my mid-teens and the writing turned in an unexpected direction. It evolved into a short story about my teenage schooldays, my-coming-of-age excitement and angst, and dredged up some previously untold and unrecorded stories. The piece ended up at 6500 words illustrated with a number of pictures. It served only a small audience of my four kids, their families and my wife. But it was extremely enjoyable and cathartic to write, the readers loved the record and the confessional nature of it and as a result, my daughter now has the tandem.

You can never be sure where a story will take you.

Early days

We've already mentioned some of the major influences on our lives. DNA can be a very interesting area to explore and many do so with the growing interest in recent years in genealogy, the tracing of ancestry. Character traits fascinate us and knowing where these come from can enlighten us about our own nature.

One valuable lead is to look at old photographs of your family. If you have older generations who can tell you about the subjects of the photographs, you will often get stories and memories flooding out. These are the start of good family histories. Old photographs enable us to see into another time and place and learn something about our predecessors, their lifestyles and their horizons. We take photography for granted with today's mobile phone capabilities, but the further back we go with photography the more expensive and unusual it was. Hence many old photographs will portray a party or birthday, wedding or some form of special occasion.

> Photographs are a frozen snapshot of history. One method to unpack the photograph and its relevance is to use the 5W's. *Who? What? Where? When? Why?* This gives the photo a sense of story.
>
> *Who* is in the photo may be an easy one but there is sometimes a random face that no one knows. There's great story telling opportunity there if you want to create a fictional piece of writing. *What* is in the photograph? Is it just people? *Where was it?* If it is in a recognisable home or room, there will be clues on the walls, perhaps other photographs or pictures, specific furniture or ornaments that you recognise. *When* was it taken, often evident from the age of the subjects. And *why?* Someone said at that precise time, "Let's take a photograph!" Films typically had few shots on them, usually from 8 up to 24. They needed to be loaded and unloaded to the camera, taken to a film processing shop to be developed and then collected. Hence, taking a photograph was an expensive and time-consuming pastime. There was a reason for the photo. What was it?

We have an old one of a group of grandparents and friends under a signpost, showing the very distant Lincolnshire village to where they were walking, a nicely-framed clue. We know we had relatives there and can guess from this that the train or bus had taken them so far and now they were walking the last leg of the journey.

'Moving photographs' were popular at seaside resorts. A cameraman would snap a photo of a group or couple

My past journey

walking down the street. The photographer would give you a card to take to a booth the next day where the photographs would be displayed alongside many others. We have examples in our family collection, some marked with a place and date – Skegness 1952, Hunstanton, 1957 and so on. What stories can you glean from these? Who did your relatives go on holiday with? How old were the children with them? They are fascinating glimpses of lives lived. For instance, it is easy to believe that with modern transportation, we are the first generation to move around freely and that our predecessors were static in one hometown. To a degree that is true but many had to move for work, or were adventurous and struck out to move overseas for better opportunities. Others had to serve in the armed forces and were shipped abroad. There is likely to be travel in your family's past. Why did they go?

But the point of these memories is to understand what previous generations have passed down to you. When a newborn arrives, everyone gathers round and immediately voices their opinions on the family resemblance to mother, father, or great uncle Albert. That's the physical side. But we think less about the character traits we inherit. You may find when thinking about your parents and further back to grandparents that certain of your own traits are identifiable. These can present you with great writing opportunities. Thank you, DNA!

Staying with early days, your first day at school is an event many remember clearly. Schools and early friends stay with us. Education can be a joy or a troubling time. How was your walk to school? Or were you taken in a four-by-four? School friends loomed large in those early days.

Adolescence offers rich pickings. This is a time of great change, physically, mentally and spiritually. Growing into adulthood brings with it many joys and also struggles. There is lots to write about the personal journey across that rickety bridge from childhood to adulthood, forging our own identity and possibly rebelling in the process.

The Art of Spiritual Writing

And your family. Parents' influences upon us are very powerful in many journeys. They are curate's eggs. Pick the bits you'd like to write about, good and bad. Again, adolescence may be a key period in this respect. And don't forget the more distant relatives. These are often fruitful material. What did your parents say of them? Did you know of such people? There may have been a favourite aunt or uncle, or someone else that looked out for you and gave you an alternative view of the world, who acted as a mentor and a foil to parental direction. These are powerful people in our personal development.

I (Richard) can also recall two distant relatives to whom we gave nicknames. We had a distant relative who lived with his family in Bath and I recall we were discussing going to visit him. A waggish teenage friend of mine on hearing this nicknamed him Uncle Plughole. The name stuck and always brought a smile to our faces when he was mentioned. Another older relative who lived a couple of streets away and did home improvements was known as Bill the Bodger. He always willingly came to do a job for my parents but was a tad ham-fisted and left a bit of a mess to clear up afterwards. Both examples were affectionate names, given in love. Such handles are a great source of writing material.

Writing those names down has sparked more random thoughts and memories in me. There was at that time Mr Tubb, the washing machine repair man, (real name), Harry, the Coalman who also delivered the Sunday papers and Mr Marshall, who managed the large Co-op shop across the road that provided all our groceries. My mother kept a weather eye on him ever since the 'maggot incident', when three of the wrigglers were spotted crawling across the newly-delivered pound of best back bacon. Hence, regular weekly bacon inspections were carried out that summer on our weekly grocery delivery. The shop was where I had a short-lived career cycling around on a grocery delivery bike. And when younger, I was dispatched there daily for

My past journey

bits and pieces as soon as I was old enough to cross the road. 'And don't forget our Divi number 4-7-4-3,' she would shout after me. The annual Co-op Dividend payout was a red-letter day in my mother's diary. I'm getting carried away and could go on …

I am surprised that all these stories have suddenly appeared. I have not thought of Mr Tubb, Harry the Coalman, or Mr Marshall for more than 30 years. Each has a strong emotional link for me from my childhood and I could now develop each one of these into a fulsome story. The writing down of those two nicknames took my writing to a new place. This is the strength of starting to write. You go to places you didn't know you were going to get to. This leads you to place where spiritual writing flourishes and they become a key starting point for developing your authentic voice.

Above are many ideas of where to find stories. Look through the microscope as these memories return. Find the small detail that sticks with you, something or someone or some event or some reason that is contained within the story. Start there.

Influencers

We've spoken a lot about early days, predominantly as these foundational years are so powerful in our formation. But the same principles that we have described above, about looking at small but significant items from your past are just as relevant as we mature.

As you review your life's spiritual journey, certain people will stick with you. You remember them more vividly. These can be specific friends, mentors, teachers or personal heroes. They may be role models such as actors, writers, comedians, special people who affected your view of life and are exceptional. They can be more specific influencers, such as coaches, counsellors, therapists or other specialists. Because they have had a personal and intimate impact in your life, there is precious material here worth exploring. You may have already recorded in writing some of your thoughts about them. If not, consider what made you value them so much.

> For me (Richard), a very small example is my French teacher in the second year of grammar school. Having been thrust from a cosy junior school into first year of high-octane education of Latin declensions and conjugations, tricksy mathematical equations, weekly memory and spelling tests, history dates, et al, it was good to meet a teacher who seemed to have a gentler more relaxed method of persuading 13-year-olds that French could be interesting. He was prepared to go off-piste, relating funny stories of his cycling adventures in France and also in one lesson recommended six novels, English, not French, that we should read. I knew I wouldn't read them all but I bought and read *1984*, *Of Mice and Men/Cannery Row*, *My Family and Other Animals*, and *Lord of the Flies*, books that have stayed with me throughout my life.
>
> I say this is a very small example but the more I think on it, the more I realise that it had a great effect on me. It set me up in two ways. First, it told me to be prepared to discover and buy my own books. Throughout my teens, I scoured the shelves in WHSmith for interesting new paperbacks. The library passed me by. I had to own it if I was going to read it. And I still have to do that. The second lesson was that you can make learning and education fun, something we strive to do in all of our courses, retreats and writing groups. These are two lessons I carry through life with me which emanated from his teaching.

My past journey

Thank you, Mr Hooper. What a spiritually-uplifting, mind-expanding and long-standing effect that one lesson had. I could write a lot more about that and already further ideas on writing about my school life are bubbling away on the stove.

The Key Ring

We've discussed earlier the idea of fishing out memories from our soup tureen. This is a powerful and useful metaphor to use to elicit random thoughts from your past. The key ring offers a different lens through which to examine your past, a means to look for other sources of writing. Our own personal key ring will hold important items, access to many vital parts of our lives. Imagine the key ring as a metaphor for accessing some key aspects of our lives. Ira Progoff, in his seminal book *At a Journal Workshop* has developed an intense and very detailed process of personal reflection and journalling. He refers to Steppingstones, what he sees as the key points or periods, recommending up to a maximum of twelve, that have occurred in your life and he gives comprehensive detail on how to explore these.

In fact, we are all conscious that our lives consist of turning points, times when the horizon shifts and something substantial or dramatic changes. These events can be self-initiated decisions, such as moving home or relocating to a new area, changing jobs, seeking a new career, going back into education, getting married, having children, to name but a few common big decisions. Or they can be thrust upon us by external forces and we are faced with traumatic circumstances such as redundancy, relationship breakdown, illness, bereavement or other events. Whether voluntary or involuntary, these are the milestones that measure out our lives. We can group these in a number of ways. Here is our way of viewing key turning points, by considering key events, key people, key feelings, key places, and key activities.

Key events. These are the times when things changed

The Art of Spiritual Writing

the *When* of the 5Ws. Think of major occasions, for instance if you got married. But don't write about all the preparations for the day. Start with a small detail. Was there amongst the wedding presents of kettles, toasters, microwaves and bedding, all now forgotten, a small token gift that moved you? Or did someone say just one thing that day that struck you and has stayed with you ever since? Was there a bit of a kerfuffle between family members? You get the general idea. Birthdays, Christmases, summers, days out, all congregate in this arena. And a simple two hours in a restaurant with special friends may be just as relevant. These are special occasions and hence fruitful areas to explore in your writing. A photo album, analogue or digital, may serve well as a memory jogger. Photo albums are time travel machines.

Key people. The *Who*. We've touched on these already. But some people will have had quite an influence, perhaps at a specific time in your journey, or probably throughout your life. We are getting into mentor and hero territory here again. These are the folks you met and remember for their impact upon your thinking and your life. You may both have moved on now, but they still hold a special place in your heart. Write about that precious time you had together. There are also the heroes you admired in film, literature, TV, or music. They count too.

Key feelings. The *Why*. You won't find these in your photo album. But you will know them. Our emotional responses in life can leave strong memories. A full list of emotions is a big task. Some key areas – happiness, love, surprise, anger, fear, disgust, jealousy and sadness give a lead into this area. There are many taxonomies of emotions online if you need more scope. What made you so cross, or gave you such a warm feeling of love? The point about writing in this area is that it can connect you quite quickly to a sense of the spiritual. It is an area where you need to let yourself go in your writing. We say more about this in the *writing for therapy* chapter, but it is important not to censor in this

My past journey

area. Get it down on paper. There is a distinctly cathartic element to writing about your feelings if you desire to explore and can let yourself go.

Key places. The *Where*. Geography is a powerful stimulant for your writing. Wherever you lived, in the country, in a town or a in a city, you will have strong memories. Recall the street where you grew up, the bedroom you had, the homes you have lived in. Did you have a favourite holiday resort, a place to which you returned regularly, somewhere that has significant spiritual meaning for you? Are you a traveller or do you prefer your home base? These are great stimuli in your writing. And again, you can reduce this to the micro-level. Look through the microscope. Read the books on your bedroom shelf, the posters on the wall. And don't just think of the visuals. There were sounds in your street. And smells and tastes. The latter are very evocative. We know folks who live near chocolate factories and sugar refineries. The air is tainted. Personally, I can recall from childhood the smell of tobacco smoke, my grandmother's lavender perfume, floor polish, a bowl of homegrown strawberries, the garden goldfish pond. We have furniture from my parents that after ten years in our house still smells of my childhood home. Every time I open a cupboard or a drawer, I am propelled back in time.

Key activities *The What*. Activities can include one-offs or recurrent activities. You can include your achievements, which may be a lifetime's work or a shorter-term achievement, a personal triumph, a one-off small event at which you volunteered or took part. They are all potential sources, rich in imagery.

Don't forget that key categories are prompts. They repeat some of the situations we have already discussed but they provide you with an alternative view and a different approach to the material you have hidden within. We have put the 5W's against these headings but these are not exclusive. The 'key places' is designated as *Where*. But as you write, your writing could lead you to the W*ho* was there, the *Why* it happened, and the *When*. The ideas is to get you writing. Let it be messy. Life is.

The recap sequence

And here is a final idea for accessing the memory banks. The recap sequence is a common device used in TV dramas. It is the short burst of montages from earlier episodes that precedes the main programme. It is there for the previous viewer or new viewer to catch up on the story. It's always fascinating to see what is included and what the editor of this short introductory piece puts in and leaves out. You can put together your own recap sequence for a short period of your life, for a special day, to bring recent past events up to the present or for whatever time period you choose. Try using it for a key point you have identified from your key ring. And note what you include and what you leave out.

Writing of darker times

And here are some more observations, this time from Eirene, on writing of our past journey.

But what do you do if you don't want to go fishing? If your ladle is likely to lift a slurry of gunge rather than sweet smelling fancies? Black gunk – tons and tons of it. Not just a few little specks but the sort of gloop you see on the news when there has been an oil spill. A veritable Torrey Canyon of effluent. You're expecting to see seagulls surfacing with sticky, blackened wings. And inside you are silently screaming with the outrage, the fury, the sadness, the grief of it all.

We've all had those times because – sorry and all that – every one of us is going to die. One day. Not on all the other days (thanks Snoopy). The even worse news is that all those we love and who we know we can't live without will too. For some of us, this may come peacefully in our sleep after a mug of hot chocolate or a sherry in our late nineties. For others it won't. And (I don't want to rub this in)

My past journey

some may have a quiet life where nothing much happens untoward, whilst others don't. Keith Richards said, 'I'm all for a quiet life. I just didn't get one', and you can't argue with that.

There are many many ways in which life can throw brickbats at us. We may be hit hard, square in the face and disfigured for life whilst our best buddy manages to dodge the blows. We may experience abuse, physical, emotional, or spiritual, relationship breakdown, addiction, unemployment, debt. Life isn't fair but it's brutally, criminally, insanely unfair for some.

And overwhelmed by the nightly news – a litany of human grief beamed into our sitting rooms, I just hunch down and ask God to be there with me, holding my hand, whispering in my ear that he's right there with us in all this chaos. In these wilderness times. Times when it's hard to pray or to reach out.

But the page is still there and the invitation to write still stands. Even if I don't think I've got it in me to write anything, I find myself writing which just goes to show that there's a spark somewhere. It's always best to be honest and write about that spark rather than making something up. (Although fiction writers seem to do all right with that.)

We are all writers and we want to do what brings us to life and gives us a reason to get up in the morning. And if we reach deep down into our-selves, we are going to find these stories that hurt, that make us blink back tears, that touch on un-named childhood terrors and rage. (This sounds a lot like the therapy chapter. Bear with. There is a point.)

And the point is this. Find your own way of writing through your darkness. It won't be mine. It won't be the same as the pal you made on your last Creative Writing course. It will be yours and yours only. Start small. Choose a story which feels shall we say, house-trained. The time you didn't get picked for the school play, but Sharon Morgan did instead. The time you went to the pictures with the boy

The Art of Spiritual Writing

you met at the bus stop and he was two-timing you all along. The time you spilled red paint all over your brand-new checked shirt.

And if your childhood was less than perfect – write that too. The time your dad flew into a rage and you kept out of the way, the time the big bullies shoved you around in the dinner queue, the time you went to church and came away scared stiff because you were convinced you weren't saved and might get run over on the way home and then where would you be?

Tell your story in your own words in just the way you want.

I like crafting the stories of my dark times. I like honing and polishing and carefully arranging every single word until it's exactly where I need it to be. (Maybe this shows my need to have some control in a world which felt out of control.) And, towards the end of the piece, I like to make sense of it now. I like to see what I've understood, to know the road on which I travelled and how I have survived. As you will too.

I grew up in a fundamentalist church which left me with an abiding fear of God ...

I am about six and sitting in one of our interminable church meetings. We are working our way through the repertoire of choruses which I know by heart. We bounce into a jolly little ditty:

'I've got the joy, joy, joy, joy down in my heart!'

Whereupon all kids present have to shout, *'WHERE?'*

'Down in my heart,' sings back the congregation.

And we dutifully holler, *'WHERE?'*

Back comes the answer, *'DOWN IN MY HEART!'* and we resignedly roar *'WHERE???'* thinking all grown-ups must be deaf.

Now there's no doubt that some of the

My past journey

> people in this church were good and godly. It's just that they didn't have much fun. Their idea of merriment was a belter of an evening singing choruses around the piano of a Saturday night, or an in-depth debate on the finer points of Leviticus. They would insist that they were 'not of the world'. 'The world' was dangerous you see, and liable to tempt the unwary into unrighteous ways which would never do. Even our telly had a stern admonishment perched on top, 'JESUS IS LORD' in case a flash of flesh or a bit of blue came on.
>
> The only time I felt joyful as a kid was when I wasn't in church.

And, over many years, my writing took me to this...

> Gradually, like the beginning of spring, a thaw began to set in and I'm no nature writer, but think hairline cracks in the ice, snow thawing and dripping from the branches of trees, the first crocuses poking through the damp earth with tiny green shoots and fragile purple flowers. I found people who knew an entirely different God and were really happy to introduce me. And I found a place to worship where I could approach this God with reverence and with awe, relishing the beauty of ritual and colour and solemnity, as well as intimacy with my Creator.

Brickbats can come at any stage of life and hit you with such intensity that they leave you broken on the ground, unable to begin to move because it hurts far too much. I was widowed in my early thirties with two tiny children ...

The Art of Spiritual Writing

> It's almost impossible when you are hurting so much to see how your crippled self can be transformed in any way at all. It felt like a life sentence. So God side-stepped all obvious routes and gave me a pass out for church services and prayer groups. Instead, he sent me people. Other people. It wasn't obvious at the time, but God wasn't worrying about a big thank-you card on his desk straightway. He doesn't always hang around in churches waiting to be spoken to, or keep silence on retreats or nudge you towards a pertinent Bible passage. He can do all these things – of course he can, but for people like me then – raging, hurt and empty, he sometimes sends people with cups of tea and scrambled eggs on toast and hugs and love.
>
> Real people with flesh and blood and bones came alongside me and listened to my desperation, held me when I was frantic, and became God's love in human form for me.

And over many years, my writing took me to this ...

> Sometimes something happens that lets the light in just a tiny little bit. It's not a floodlight or a spotlight or a beacon – it doesn't suddenly illumine everything with an overwhelming brightness. It's more of a glimmer with a promise of radiance to come.
>
> Maybe all it needs is a just a small crack to let the light in – a different way of seeing things, an alternative view of the past. This anguish has been around for so long that I forget to question why it was ever so in the first place. It just is. It's

My past journey

> a given. These are the facts of how it happened. And if they rub relentlessly inside, if the wound is occasionally touched so deeply and the pain so excruciating that I want to curl up in a ball and weep and weep for the sheer agony of it all – then that's how it is. Because the past can't be altered. The past can't be rewritten and relived. It is as it is.
>
> Except – except – and this is where the light gets in through the crack – maybe this other way of looking at things can change them. Not the set-in stone facts about what happened – but the way in which I consider myself. The way in which I remember that time and the decisions I made and the conclusions I came to.
>
> For years and years, I have felt so bad. I let you down. I failed you. I've felt so guilty, haunted, by the memories of what I did and didn't do.
>
> Then, I was given a lifeline. I was told that I didn't let you down. I did the best I could with the understanding I had at that time. My only intention was to help. I need to forgive myself for being young, for not knowing what to do and for not knowing what was going to happen next.
>
> I imagine our precious daughter, facing this, she now, the age I was then – and doing the same. And I would say to her, 'Well done. You did your best. It was all you could do. And it's okay.'
>
> And that's how the light gets in.

It can take years to percolate. Take time to find your rhythm. Do what works for you. Stories are surfacing in your head. Let them loose on the page. Write when you can. I'm best in the morning, as so many of us are who call ourselves writers. My study invites me in, my own special space, crammed full of family photographs and of course, shelves of books.

I sit at my desk, open my laptop, and begin my

diversionary tactics. Beginning is the hardest part. There's nothing there. But nothing turns to something and soon the words are dancing on the page. I am connected and I am happy. Even though I'm writing the tough stuff, I am happy.

And don't forget that you can write right in the middle of hard times too. I found immense relief in crafting a piece in the moment when we were facing a storm that we simply didn't know how to weather ...

> When you don't know what to do, it's best to do something. Mooching around pretending to be busy by moving a stack of ironing from one end of the bed to the other or suddenly playing at gardening, coming over all Charlie Dimmock and dead-heading roses doesn't work. It has to be authentic. It has to have a purpose. You have to do something by actually doing something rather than doing nothing and pretending it's something.
>
> When you are in limbo-land as we are at the moment, waiting for a hospital appointment it's best to keep doing something. As my priest-friend said to me last week 'do something nice for yourselves'. She didn't say 'do nothing for yourselves'.
>
> So, we are having days out. Along with most of the other silver pounders across the country, we are rocking up at retail outlets, walking along canal paths and lunching in aspirational cafes all across the county. We know every jacket potato filling there is. We even copied one and brought it home. We marvel at the array of tat on offer at places where you can waste your money on souvenirs of a right good day out, stuffing your shopping bags full of Derbyshire fudge and cushion covers with a picture of Arkwright's Mill. Although at one exhibition, there was a lovely lady selling her home-made silver jewellery and my husband insisted on

My past journey

> treating me saying, 'There's a lot going on right now', which made me want to cry.

Just remember, no one knows (or much cares) if you write or not. But you do. And if your writing helps you, just a teeny bit, to get through those times when the world tilts on its axis and you can't breathe with the awfulness of it all – then it's worth it. It's worth that word on the paper – that sentence, that paragraph. That declaration of life saying, 'I am here. And I can write. And I will survive!'

So, we've been talking about our past – our past which is full of stories – even those stories we'd rather forget and which give us a little shiver through our psyche as we dare to recall them. We remember them, sometimes in stark and horrific slow motion, sometimes with the clarity of a Disney movie in glorious technicolour. Sometimes we add bits or take bits away. Or make bits up. It doesn't matter – they are still our stories and they matter.

And we know that we can't change the bare bones of these stories. They are what they are and they happened. But you can change what you do with them. Writing has the power to do this. The power to change, if not the beginning of your story, the ending. You can finish the story just how you want to. With forgiveness. With resolution. With acceptance. With love.

And the past becomes the present in the past in the puff of a breath, a blink of an eye, a dash of a second. I'm sitting here right now, writing about stories and those things that matter and realising that this moment matters too. This moment is my story and I'm already remembering it. So, our past becomes our present. And writing in our present can bring enormous relief. It can also bring gratitude and joy and healing and wholeness. And it will bring that sharp pain which tugs and gnaws at your innards as you live this moment, and just won't let you go. Live it, as you write this moment, whatever it brings. Write in your Daily Pages. Write in your journal. Free write as if you were eight years old and have a shiny new blank exercise book to fill. Above all, write. It's you that you are writing and you matter.

And just remember – if writing this stuff triggers painful memories that are too hard to handle – get help. Talk to a friend, a minister, a counsellor, a good listener. Don't try to cope with it all by yourself. We are not alone.

We have covered a lot of ground here on the past journey. There are a host of ideas you can use to help you access suitable material to write about. Too much? If so, explore the ideas of immediate interest to you. Start with those and see where they take you to.

There is a summary map below as a reminder of the main areas covered. Is there a topic that speaks to you here? Pick and mix, and if it isn't working, try another. And remember the soup tureen. There are plenty of memories to fish out. Dip the ladle in and go fishing!

Writing prompts

Redraft your story from Chapter 1 – write as you can, not as you can't
Take your rough draft. Look at the 5Ws we covered in this chapter, the *Who What Where When Why* of this story. Consider each of these and start to enrich your story as a consequence. Have you a title for the story?

Now there's an idea…
As you read this chapter, did you get an idea for a story? If

My past journey

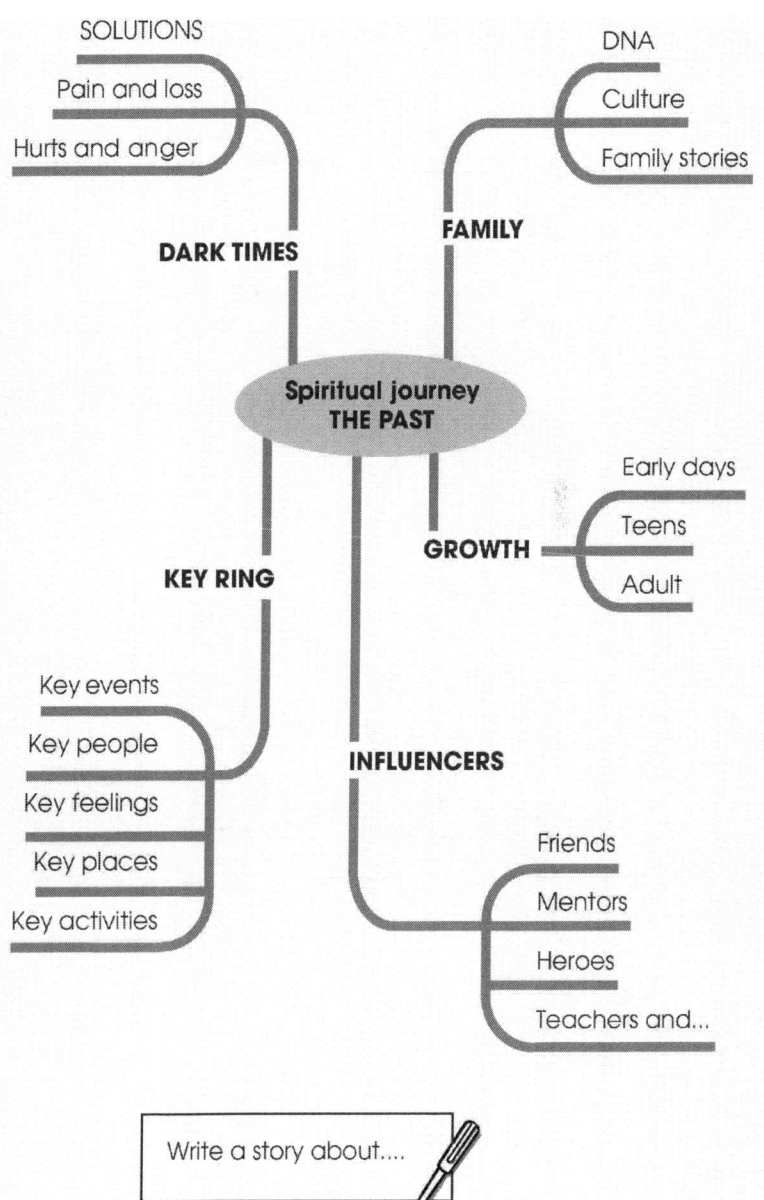

The Art of Spiritual Writing

so, start to write it down. Allow yourself a page and a half of A4 and see where it takes you to. When you have finished it, read it through aloud to yourself and imagine the reader and what they may want to know. Redraft where necessary.

Old photographs
Somewhere you will have old family photographs. Pick one of these. Take time to absorb the detail of it, the more detail the better. Review it with an eagle-eye. Who is in it, who isn't, the facial expressions, the background detail. Write a story about that photograph.

Trigger ideas
Write about one of the following. Start with a page and see how far you go.

- Our street
- First job
- My favourite book
- So funny!
- I was proud of that
- Teatime
- Teenage bedroom
- A holiday to remember
- Meeting God
- Aunts and Uncles
- My best friend
- Big embarrassment
- A popular family story
- The dog
- Next door
- Nice surprise

CHAPTER 3

Present times

There is no greater agony than bearing an untold story inside you.

Maya Angelou

Writing, to me, is simply thinking through my fingers.

Isaac Asimov

What's on your mind today? Every day as you wake your brain serves up a menu of items for you to address. It's your personal nagometer, chuntering away at you, and covers all bases. If you are employed, the work basket will be first up, laden with actions – forthcoming meetings, emails, phone calls, activities, visits, all part of your daily agenda. And then follows the personal basket – the dental appointment, the car service, there's no milk, the big shop to do. All a part of life's rich tapestry. All salient but diverting thoughts and we'll look at dealing with these later in freewriting and other techniques.

The tree of life

But let us look now at our present life in bigger terms. There's another basket of stuff that your brain is telling you about. This one contains the more important yet non-urgent concerns, things you need to or would like to sort out and haven't yet done so. That is often because they are too big to sort out in a day, or maybe you have no idea how to sort them. These are the medium-term

The Art of Spiritual Writing

issues of life – our dissatisfactions, the parts we need to heal, the problems we need to address and put right, the unmanaged and unexpressed feelings we have, an awkward person we are dealing with. Or things we want to achieve, aspirations and desires, as yet unexpressed. Such situations may well affect our wellbeing and need our attention.

They are the unresolved. And for you, the writer, such materials are like the Christmas gift catalogue. They offer a rich source of ideas to explore. And as they are your own personal issues, they are likely to possess a deep spiritual interest and meaning for you. You have here a handful of gold dust to write about.

And remember that we have now moved from the past, that period in which things cannot be undone. We are now considering the present period of our spiritual journey. This is the stepping stone from your past into your future. Decisions taken now can have effects upon your future. That's stating the blatantly obvious. Nevertheless, as we write about our present situations, it is a worthwhile thought to bear in mind. Because articulating our current situation and circumstances to writing can well influence the decisions we take. Writing in the here and now is a time to reflect upon what is and what is not and writing is the powerful means at our disposal to do this.

A useful tool is to think about your life as a tree, with a number of branches representing the various aspects of your life. You can slice and dice this in a thousand ways. For the purposes of simplicity, this is our division of some of the key aspects of living. As you work with this, be prepared to add any of your own important and personally significant categories that you want to consider. For instance, under the heading of 'leisure', if you are a keen sports person, you may want to drill down a level and review this in detail, considering all your activities and achievements, where you are currently with your fitness and how you will modify your goals and aspirations as you grow older. Or

Present times

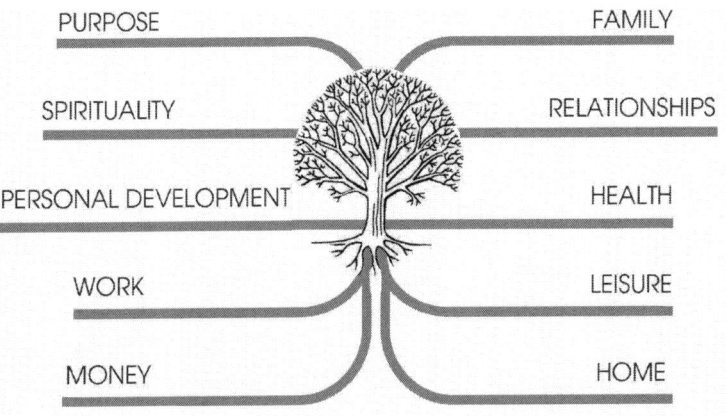

you can start from scratch and sketch out your own tree. We all know life does not subdivide neatly into categories. All of these are interdependent with one another. You pull a lever in one area and it changes something elsewhere. And if you make really big changes, such as moving house to a new area, then it can impinge on many other areas of life.

The tree gives you the opportunity to explore some the major branches of your life. It is often true that until we articulate our thoughts in writing, we don't really know what we think about the matter under consideration. It can therefore be a powerful route to self-discovery. And you may get quite passionate in your writing. That's fine, let it all hang out. Honest and open writing can be very cathartic. And it can be most revealing, illuminating enlightenment appearing on the page before your eyes. Read through the categories in the tree. This is an activity worthy of repeating again and again. It often can spawn other avenues that you really didn't think mattered too much to you. It is a marvellous way to vocalise your innermost thinking. And it is a wonderful way to practise your art of spiritual writing. These subject matters are invariably situations that mean much to you. As Gustave Flaubert said, 'The art of writing is the art of discovering what you believe.'

Encouraging the muse

Nothing coming to you? We cannot force the writing to come. Inspiration is a capricious master and creativity a flighty mistress. To encourage this fickle couple to come to your aid, a useful technique is to read a couple of pages of an inspirational writer whose work you admire before you set pen to paper. This pump priming is a remarkably effective catalyst to get your pen moving.

Another very well tested formula is to go and take a walk. *Solvitur ambulando*, a Latin phrase translating as 'it is solved by walking', works very effectively. If you read biographies of writers and how they write, this need to get up and change the activity away from writing is a common theme. Personally, we find it very effective when we hit the buffers halfway through a piece of work. The solution doesn't need to be a five-mile yomp across the hills, just a short walk across the park or somewhere green does the trick. It sets one's mind off in new directions and lets the outside world in. Set yourself a task to think about as you set off and your subconscious will work away on your writing project for you.

You may also find you have a better time of day for writing. Some are regular morning writers, some in the evenings, or just spasmodic bursts when the inspiration strikes. You will know what rhythm suits you. As noted earlier, there's no guaranteed best time other than to say quite a lot of people like that early morning slot. If you are interested in the subject, Mason Currey, in his book, *Daily Rituals, How Great Minds Make Time, Find Inspiration and Get to Work*, looks at the routines of over 160 artists writers, musicians and other creatives and what works for them.

Present times

The daily round

Be alert. There is writing material around every corner all day long. Keep your ears and eyes open. As Oron Scott Card said, 'Everybody walks past a thousand story ideas every day. The good writers are the ones who see five or six of them. Most people don't see any.' We call it *writer's ear*. Frequently when we are in public places – on a train, a bus, in a café or bar, restaurant or shop, one of us will mouth to the other silently *'writer's ear!'* and indicate with eye movements the direction of the overheard conversation. Honestly, we never deliberately eavesdrop. It is simply that people do talk inadvertently loudly in public places. And often these are deep and meaningful conversations because they are important life-related stories being told by one person to another. There is much of interest for us as spiritual writers. There is, of course, the exception, the muppet on the train who insists on talking loudly into his mobile to ensure the whole carriage knows about how important his current deal is and how he's sorting it all out single-handed.

> A top writing tip from me (Richard) is to use a thesaurus. Having studied languages earlier in life, I've always had one on my desk. For instance, I wanted a word more evocative than *idiot* to describe the above scenario. My word processing thesaurus is too shy to even search on the word idiot when I was looking for the right word. My copy of the Concise Oxford Thesaurus gave me 63 alternatives, including *muppet*. That's an amazing selection. A thesaurus will enrich your writing and we'll look at other methods of doing this later on when we look at metaphors.

The Art of Spiritual Writing

These conversations, titbits, observations and the general background chatter of life are great hunting grounds for writing material. Many of our short articles and humorous pieces are generated from such sources. What did you see and hear? Your readers will be interested to know.

This is also a great source to capture real voices if you need dialogue for your writing. The language is often salty, local, short, unfinished sentences, barmy ideas, staccato verbiage. Situational comedy draws deeply on these sources. Take such ideas and develop them. You can spin what was a real event and with creative non-fiction, add to it to give it more kudos. Again, comedians are good at this – exaggerating and embellishing. And to be honest, we all do this. When we have told the same favourite story over and over again, we embellish. The fish we caught grows bigger each time, that crucial meeting we had to get to London to attend and made it with just ten minutes to spare. After a few tellings, we walked in just as the meeting was starting. I wonder how much that bowl of chips of Marco Pierre White's costs now?

The writer's notebook

The missing link in all of this writer's ears and eyes is remembering it. Have a notebook with you and write it down.

Herein is the source material for future writing. This is your stash of golden nuggets. Ideas flash through our minds like express trains. You hear them coming and then in a split second they have disappeared down the track. Such thoughts are often so valuable. Catch them while you can. Just a few words on a piece of paper and you have them saved.

Anything that is worthy of note should go in here. A snatch of conversation, some gossip, a relevant article seen in the paper, a scribbled note of the first few lines of a piece you are planning to write, the first line or meter of a poem.

Ideas also come at strange times. The liminal space on

Present times

waking and dozing off often yield ideas, as does sleep and dreams. Many keep a bedside notebook for such flashes of inspiration. We've had many things come and go in the night, lost forever. Your mind says to you, 'Don't bother to wake up. Go back to sleep, I'll remember this for you.' It doesn't. As Saul Bellow observed, 'You never have to change anything you got up in the middle of the night to write.'

On driving the 30 miles to a local city one Saturday morning, we were discussing our writing and had a brilliant idea come to us. We were very excited. We must write that up when we get home, we said. We didn't. A few weeks later we were reminiscing and questioned each other sheepishly on what the idea was. Neither of us could remember. Neither of us. We said it will come back to us in a day or two. It never did and it never has. Gone!

Write it down. Use whatever works for you. Our personal method is a number of small and large notebooks. Some use notebooks, some mobile phones. Anne Lamott in *Bird by Bird* tells how she uses index cards as her recording process. 'I have index cards and pens all over the house – by the bed, in the bathroom, in the kitchen, by the phones, and I have them in the glove compartment of my car. I carry one with me in my back pocket when I take my dog for a walk.'

> It's horses for courses. For instance, I (Richard) keep two ideas journals, one posh A4 one at home and a small notebook I'll stick in my pocket for creative days out or when I go on holiday. I also do a project file if I'm developing a big writing idea or developing a course. I do also keep index cards if I'm researching a big piece of writing, so that I can find that nugget of a quote or can sort the various themes into chapters. To repeat the mantra, whatever works for you.

The Art of Spiritual Writing

The noting down of ideas is as old as the hills. We came across the idea of the Commonplace Book only recently. We are indebted to the Rev Dr Alan Flintham who came to share his writing process with our writing group recently and brought along his commonplace book. It is for him a treasure trove of ideas that help to fire and inspire his writing. Commonplace books have a long history and in days when knowledge was scarce and hard to come by, they were a repository for recording useful information. They were favoured by writers, artists, scientists and many others. Wikipedia's page *The Commonplace Book* records a detailed history of them. Books were published on how to keep these and some Commonplace Books have been published.

My 'posh' A4 notebook could count as one. I use that mainly for lengthy articles and am particularly drawn to obituaries of those I admire. I mention these because they are masterful examples of short stories of lives lived, the edited highlights.

> When I (Richard) tell friends how much I enjoy a good obituary, I often get a startled sidelong glance thrown in my direction. But I've always thought of them as an art form, catching the essence of a person's life. I prefer to think of them more as their spiritual walk, as they often capture the hills and hollows, the joys and sorrows of a life. I was therefore delighted to read the following in the foreword to a collection of obituaries, entitled *Lives Less Ordinary*, edited by Nigel Farndale, Obituaries Editor of the *Times* newspaper:
>
> 'Far from being morbid or gloomy, they are often life affirming, entertaining, too, full of colour, felicities and, more often than you would imagine, kindly humour. And in a world of social

> media snippets, they are not only "long form", as we nowadays like to say when we mean "long", but they also have a satisfying narrative arc, with pleasing cadences and a natural, cradle-to-grave, beginning, middle and end.'
>
> See Signposts for more information on obituaries.

When people struggle to keep their word count down for short stories, I often cite the obituary as a prime example of succinct writing.

So there you have it. These are some well tried and tested ways to record your thoughts and ideas. Write it down otherwise the material will disappear. The more you write down or post into your notebooks, the greater your collection of source material.

It matters not where and how you record things, on cards, in books on your phone, on table napkins, the important matter is to get it down. This is your commonplace book for all your writing prompts. If you keep such a notebook, you will have a treasury of information to spark your imagination at those times when the Muse has gone walkabout.

The bigger-than moments

And let us not forget that we are writing a spiritual journey. There will be times when you have felt something bigger than you, the *bigger-than* moments as we call them, the numinous times and the transcendent events of mystery. As Pierre Teilhard de Chardin is reputed to have said 'We are not human beings having a spiritual experience. We are spiritual beings having a human experience.' When you have them, write about them. I (Richard) can recall three immediately and reproduce them below as I made contemporaneous notes on them all at the time.

The Art of Spiritual Writing

The first was our car crash on the motorway in 2014. An articulated lorry pulled out of lane one directly into the side of us in lane two. He just hadn't seen us. At the sound of grinding metal on the side of our car at 60 mph, I thought we were dead. The collision threw our car in front of the lorry and up a thirty-metre bank. My whole being in that instant was focused on steering that car. My feet leave the pedals as I hunch forward to wrestle with the steering wheel. All I can see is a sea of grass rushing up at me. It feels like the tyres have blown. The rocks are scraping on the bottom of the car. A few seconds later the upward arc flattens and we are suddenly leaning sideways at a dangerously steep angle. Oh, my God, the car is going to roll. I manage to turn it back down the embankment towards the road. We are gathering speed, heading back to the motorway. My extreme panic now is to find the brake pedal. I hadn't realised my feet had left the pedals and were braced on to the floor. Where the f**k is it? My feet can't find it. Oh, my God, where is it? Where is it? I find it. Will they work? We bounce over a gulley and on to the hard shoulder. The brakes work. We stop. There is a microsecond of silence. 'Get out quick, we're alive,' I shout to my wife. We tumble out miraculously and flop onto the grass embankment, quivering wrecks. I try to dial 999. In shock, I can't get my phone and fingers to coordinate. A kind couple who saw it all run up and take over. Amazingly they are on their way to visit their mum 150 miles away, who lives just two streets from mine. Ambulance and police arrive.

    The traffic policeman advised me later to buy a lottery ticket that night. 'Not many people walk

Present times

away from one like that, sir,' he said. That night, we told a neighbour about the lottery ticket story. She put three through our door the following morning. We didn't win. But we already had. I wrote it up later as an article entitled *Did you ever meet God?* The final sentence read, 'That's when we met God, that sunny April afternoon on the motorway.' And we had. We both felt God's hand upon us as we walked away from a near fatal crash with no major injuries.

The second was at 4.40 am one morning. I had a bad cold and couldn't sleep and was downstairs doing the crossword. There was a knocking at the door, except it wasn't at the door, it was on the inside of my skull. It was my Mum's knock. She was in a nursing home with early-stage dementia. 'You there, duck?' It was what she'd say on entering a room. 'I'm going now. I'm all right. I've had enough. I'm okay.' I burst out crying. And I was convinced she had died. I went back to bed and awaited the early morning call from the nursing home. It didn't come.

The experience was so real that it brought me great comfort at a time when we were losing her to dementia, particularly the words, 'I'm okay.' A year later my son was over from New Zealand and was going to see his nan. To prepare him for her dementia, I told him this story. I was shocked that he was not surprised by this spiritual sensation. He said he'd had firm premonitions in his mind when both his grandfathers had died. In one case, he heard the next morning, in the other, 10 minutes later. Numinous events.

The third is a ghost story. We rented a cottage for a holiday in the countryside. The main bedroom at the end of the landing felt so spooky when we arrived that we didn't feel comfortable

> to sleep in it but opted for a smaller room nearer to the stairs. We both felt very unsettled. We slept with the landing light on and walked downstairs to the loo in the night together. We are not easily frightened but this felt creepy. Later that week, we both read in the visitor's book that a couple of other guests had commented the house was haunted. We didn't mention it to one another for fear of spooking each other but as soon as we got in the car to head home, we both breathed a sigh of relief and burst forth with stories of our fears and feelings.
>
> I told this story to many people afterwards at home and at work. Rather than ridicule or leg-pulling, which is what I had expected, I was amazed by the number of stories others had to tell of such transcendent experiences. The ones from work surprised me. These were engineers, practical, logical, balanced individuals with their feet firmly on the ground. Some of their stories were far more poignant than mine. 'We are spiritual beings having a human experience.'

The *bigger-than* moments. They will always tell a rich deep story. We have both had very disturbing periods of time in our lives before we met. When we discuss these, with one another, we wonder how we got through such traumatic times and acknowledge with hindsight that God had carried us across those traumatic periods and brought the right people forward to walk with us. They were *bigger-than* moments.

As I said earlier, I have a personal test that I apply to my own writing when I wonder if it is truly *spiritual* writing. I reread it on completion. If I get a lump in my throat or a tear in my eye, I know it is good. I then pass it over to my editor-in-chief, Mrs Palmer, to read. If I've had the tear, I know she will say, 'Wow, that hits the spot!'. If your own writing moves you, it will move others. It happened to me just now, retelling the story of the car crash.

Eirene now takes over the baton to the end of this chapter to talk about the processes of taking in and giving out in our present walk.

Taking in and giving out

'You can't push the river.' It's one of those quotable quotes that trips off the tongue. People nod their heads wisely on hearing it and say sagely, 'You can't step into the same river twice.' That river has a lot to answer for. It seems to know more about where I'm going than I do.

Writing is like that river. It's a process. 'Trust the process', is the mantra. Three little words bandied around in every creative writing workshop. Trust the darned process. Don't try and write a bestseller by tomorrow afternoon. The Muse will come when it comes. Trust that given time and space and lots of nurture and watering, the garden will grow. See! Aren't we just chock full of helpful and succinct metaphors.

Writing is a way of both taking in and giving out. Writing enables me to function. It helps me to breathe. It helps me to take in light and life and air and sustenance. It enables me to turn my face towards the sun and drink in its healing rays and bask for just a little while in its warmth and glow. I take time out on my spiritual coast-to-coast walk (check the metaphor again) and maybe have a sit down in a nice shady glade and have a sleep and a snack.

But writing can also be a way of giving out. I wrote for a long time for a church magazine and often had people come up to me in the aisles at Sainsbury's and tell me how much my article had helped them that week. They would unburden themselves, sometimes alarmingly, over the mushrooms and tomatoes. My piece had touched them inside – which is the place I wrote it from – and I am all at once humbled and challenged by the effect that putting it out there has had.

Taking in and giving out. We need both to be upright balanced people because if we only did one, we would tilt over and likely crash to the ground. Life is best lived in balance. There are any number of magazines and helpful newspaper articles telling us how to live our best-balanced life and they're not wrong. They tend to major most on a work/life balance and it must be hard to achieve this if you have a two hour commute every day and a two- and four-year-old waiting for you when you get home. But writing will find a way. Like a leak in the kitchen, it will seep its way into every little nook and cranny of available space. But it's obviously easier if you're retired. I've done both, so I know.

Taking in

So, writing can be one way we take in. One way in which we touch base with ourselves. One way in which we carve out a fraction of time to call our own and put ourselves down on paper. Don't worry if it's two hours or two minutes. It all counts. Just do it. Have a notebook and a pen to hand and put yourself onto the paper even if your to-do list is longer than the PCC minutes. At one of our writing workshops, we asked people to just write words – one word, two words, maybe a sentence. And they could do that. They weren't sure they were writers but they could write words. As Chloe Neill wrote in *Firespell*, 'You string some letters together, and you make a word. You string some words together, and you make a sentence, then a paragraph, then a chapter. Words have power.'

There may be other ways in which you can take in too. Mine are singing and walking. Don't neglect these other ways as its only by taking in that we can give out. Think about where you are fed. Prayer, meditation, creativity, painting, crocheting, being outside. Make sure you get enough of what brings you to life to sustain you.

Present times

And consider your support networks. If you have them, use them.

And I know, I know it's easier at some stages of life than others. But try for what you can because you count and you matter.

> Both of us frequently find ourselves talking about the things that bring us to life. We call these pursuits *spiritual serotonin*, the stuff we do that brings us pleasure and relaxation, that causes those lovely jolly little neurotransmitters to flood through us, spreading joy and happiness. We were talking about this one day as this book was forming and the next morning in the wee small hours, the following unexpectedly nagged me to get up and write it down:
>
> 'I awoke thinking of all the things that bring people to life. A list started to rush out of me, darting from here to there, eddying back, then surging forward, then back again. I got up and wrote out the jumble of the pre-dawn list that was churning in my mind.
>
> I realised that many of these interests were either about gaining knowledge, developing skills, or solving problems. But they were also primarily about the excitement, curiosity and satisfaction of doing what we love to do. They were about our passions. Some were outdoor, some were indoor, some interior personal interests, others external pursuits involving other people.
>
> The list seemed to kick off with the generic home-based elements – such as family, faith, social circle, job, voluntary work, home, gardening, pets, sport and arts. All of these groups contain very many sub-categories and specialities and my thinking seemed to shift down into these

specific areas. It was totally random. What struck home was that the list was very eclectic. Some of the subjects I loved and were my own personal choices. Others left me cold. It was clear that one man's meat was another man's poison. (There's a metaphor if ever I heard one.)

The list started with amateur dramatics, listening to music, beekeeping, yoga, photography, local history, painting, sewing, teashops, politics, DIY, interior design, embroidery, cookery, fishing, visiting museums, real ale, dancing, car renovation, travel, environmental issues, collecting, video games and antiques.

I went downstairs to get some breakfast but the tape wouldn't stop playing – learning a new language, flower arranging, playing a musical instrument, railways, mind maps, drawing mandalas, quizzes, choral singing, country walks, music festivals, computer programming, the gym, social media, outward bound, baking, cycling, architecture, fashion, conservation, camping, genealogy, film and TV, board games, astronomy, crossword puzzles, birdwatching, scrapbooking, journalling, poetry, reading, and oh, of course, writing. An amazing colourful tapestry of interests, hobbies and pastimes was revealing itself. Interestingly, as soon as I started to write, the tape finally stopped playing.

Tell the world what you know about matchbox labels, growing fuchsias, the Midland Railway or the 1964 Olympic Games. Whatever it is that brings us to life personally is worth writing about. It will engender good spiritual writing because it comes from a deep place within and it makes us glow. Our enthusiasm and knowledge will shine through. But more than that. We shall find there is a ready readership, because those

> who share our passions will be delighted to read about them.

Giving out

Then, there is the other side of the see-saw. The giving out. Most of us do this all the time without thinking about it overmuch. However, sometimes we come across people in our lives who are just plain self-centred and want to do everything for themselves. The loving response is to feel compassion for their warped and narrow frame of mind which won't leave them with a lot of friends in their old age, and maybe pray for them. That's the loving response. The not-so-loving doesn't need to be spelled out, but can involve much prayer for change in ourselves as we battle with resentment and fury at another's lack of love. And maybe forgiveness for ourselves for our willingness to beat ourselves up for being human.

Some things we do are non-negotiable though, like caring for an aged mum who lives alone and simply can't manage by herself. It doesn't matter how many phone calls and visits she needs – she is a priority. End of. But other things can be reviewed now and then. I was once doing a job for the diocese which I wasn't sure whether to give up or not. And maybe I was a teeny-weeny bit reluctant to give up the so-called 'status' that went with it. But I wanted to do other things and this job felt as if it was getting in the way. My priest-friend said, reasonably to me, 'You either do it for ever, or you set a finishing date,' which, when you think about it, said it all. So, I set a finishing date and gave myself a big wide-open space to step into and discover new things about myself after we'd had the leaving do and the speeches and some cake.

So – look at your commitments. Those minutes you have to type for the Church Fabric Fund, your shift at the food bank, your turn on leafleting every house in the village for the Christmas services. I'm not saying leave others in the

The Art of Spiritual Writing

lurch and I'm not saying don't do things for other people. I'm saying review what you do and make sure your needs are in there somewhere. Give things up if you want to and you can and make yourself some open space. You may even fill it with writing.

And just give yourself a pass-out on the guilt that can come with doing something you enjoy. Writing can feel like an indulgence. It can feel like you are tap-tap-tapping away at your laptop whilst the world is burning. But the world needs writers. The world needs people who can say it like it is, who aren't afraid to write the challenging and unsettling things. Who aren't afraid to pray on paper. The world has enough achievers and politicians and warmongers and people who want to turn back the boats. It needs more compassion and understanding and arms across the shoulders leading towards a welcome. And that is what writing can do. Because it can change you from the inside out, and it can change people on the outside too, if you share it.

And I filled the wide-open space I was discovering with something which fed me, and brought me to life and enabled me to breathe in goodness and wholeness. And I just had to write about it...

> I was asked a while back by my cathedral church if I'd like to join the server's team. And I said 'yes' – mainly because I like the word. Serving. Jesus came as a servant, didn't he? I couldn't go far wrong in wanting to serve. Okay, I know that those from a different church background may say I could serve better in a soup kitchen or a food bank but it doesn't stop me doing those things as well. There are many words in our stretchy English language which have lots of different meanings and serving is one of them. Also, my church experiences had never put me in the way

Present times

of servers before and I wanted to travel around a bit on my spiritual journey.

I was kitted out with a white alb (about a foot lopped off the bottom because I'm somewhat vertically challenged) and shown how to arrange my amice around my neck like a medieval monk (I'd never heard of an amice either. Nothing to do with rodents). Tying my girdle proved to be a trial and I had to practise with YouTube for a few days before I got my knot right. Amazing what you can find on YouTube. (Thanks, Daniel.) Then I was let loose on the procession on the Feast of Christ the King. I had all on keeping hold of my candle, negotiating steps and not getting in anyone's way. Although at one point, I took a wrong turn and collided with the bloke carrying the cross who was very nice about it and didn't even mention his crushed toes afterwards.

And what I found, when I finally stood completely still, was a place of peace within whilst around me, the Eucharist was celebrated. It was as though there was a kernel of serenity tucked away deep inside which I'd not been able to access before. I was expected to do nothing but stand and I wondered at this new inner calm and harmony, healed by just being and receiving, a truly numinous event.

The cynical part of me can kick and scream all she likes, but I know that I have that place within, where I can touch the peace of God. And ask her to hold my hand as I negotiate those steps with my candle.

Writing is like breathing. You have to breathe in and out. Take in, give out. It's the stuff of life.

Start your writing fitness today!

The present. This is a great place to write about. The past is reflective, the future is prospective. But there is a passion and urgency in writing about the present. Here is your opportunity to write in the present tense about what *is* happening. Not in the past tense about what *did* happen. Not in the future tense about what *might* happen.

It's like going to the gym. You can't go to the gym last week. You can't go to the gym next week. Until next week gets here and then it's the present. So if you want to build up your muscles, you have to do it now. Building up your writing muscle is no different. Start writing now. Getting something down on paper marks the beginning of your writing fitness regime.

There is a summary map below of some of the main aspects of this chapter on present times followed by the usual writing prompts for suggested topics. Here's the opportunity to pick an activity that speaks to you immediately, at this very point of your present time.

Writing prompts

The tree of life

Remember the tree. Did you reflect upon it? if not, turn back to the diagram and read through the categories in the tree diagram. Reflect upon one of these areas that is top of your mind at present. Now *talk to yourself* about this in writing. Set off for the magical one and a half pages of A4 and see where you get to. Write purposefully, vigorously and openly about the matter. This is an exercise worth revisiting regularly.

Present times

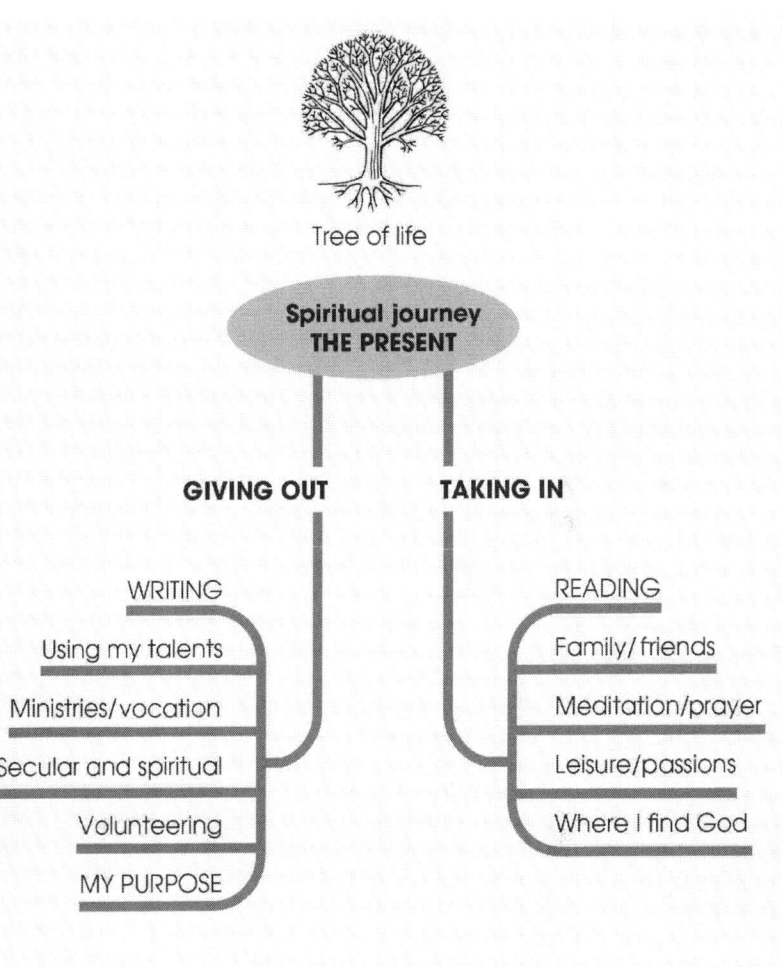

Tree of life

Spiritual journey THE PRESENT

GIVING OUT

- WRITING
- Using my talents
- Ministries/vocation
- Secular and spiritual
- Volunteering
- MY PURPOSE

TAKING IN

- READING
- Family/friends
- Meditation/prayer
- Leisure/passions
- Where I find God

What brings me strength? Write about it...

Your life balance
Pick something that is out of balance for you at present. Use the 'Taking in' and the 'Giving out' or as we like to call it, the in-box and the out-tray in the map above if you are short of ideas. Write about your feelings on the matter. Try to write quickly and instinctively. Get it down on paper. You can edit it later.

A small thing
Have you had any thoughts on small matters arise during reading this chapter? Start with a small item of memory and write down your recollections on this. See where it leads you.

Numinous moments
Recall a time when you sensed something bigger at work in your life, short or long term, large or small.

CHAPTER 4
Looking forward

Consult not your fears but your hopes and your dreams. Think not about your frustrations, but about your unfulfilled potential. Concern yourself not with what you tried and failed in, but with what it is still possible for you to do.
Pope John XXIII

So, what's next? Do you want to know? It is a theme that intrigues most of us. We were once at a spiritual retreat where the last session asked of us, 'What does God and life have in store for you next?' The woman beside us was paying rapt attention awaiting her turn to speak, as we went round the group of a dozen of us. She was 93 years-old and still questioning. We all want to know.

We are intensely curious about our futures. Certain people have made a good living since ancient times out of this curiosity. Think psychics and fortune-tellers – also clairvoyants, crystal-gazers, prophets, seers, oracles, soothsayers, augurs, diviners, sibyls, palmists and palm-readers and spaewifes (the Scottish word) (Thank you, *Concise Oxford Thesaurus*. Just saying.) And those ancient words in that list tell us that this is not a recent phenomenon but an age-old human desire to know the way ahead. You'll be pleased to know that we are not suggesting reading tea leaves or stargazing but we shall be considering how writing can help us to consider what our future may look like.

The Art of Spiritual Writing

When we ask the five-year-old what they want to be when they grow up, and hear either an artist, an astronaut or more likely the latest Disney fairy godmother or superhero, they haven't a lot of information to go on. But as adults, our spiritual journeys have already provided numerous clues and pointers that can inform our potential future.

We've looked thus far at the past journey. Whilst it remains unchangeable, it has left us many gifts, including the development of certain skills, knowledge, viewpoints and behaviours. We've then progressed to consider the present and the writing opportunities that the present brings to us. And it is at this stage in our journeys that we are in a position where we can make changes. What we decide to do now in life, any changes we make, and how we use this situation going forward, will affect our futures.

Lifestyle advice and choices abound in newspapers magazines, and online. More exercise, better food, more sleep, less stress. Most of us are getting pretty stressed by the idea that we are not making enough changes to keep up with the crowd. In addition to all the health advice, every company is telling us that their products will make us younger, happier and more successful. Our marketing friends know that we want to improve our lives and prospects and the promise of a brighter smile with their new toothpaste with more added tooth-whitening chemicals is just the ticket for a guaranteed happier future. It promises more sunshine-filled holidays with lots of glamorous friends.

If your current toothpaste brand is bugging you at present, write about it. Write about anything that you are passionate about. But we'd like to think that there are more pressing, interesting and personally relevant topics for you to write about than toiletries.

There is often a golden thread that runs through our lives. Often, it can be indiscernible at the early stages of our journey but one that with age becomes a clearer path, weaving in and out through the complex and messy tapestry of our past. As Herbert Alphonso says in his book,

Looking forward

Discovering Your Personal Vocation, 'Are you surprised that your personal vocation has been present all through your life history?'

Vocation can be a bit of a startling word, conjuring up pictures of lawyers, doctors, research scientists and politicians slavishly devoting their whole lives to exceptionally good works. But it can be any activity or pursuit where a person has a skill, specific knowledge or aptitude. For instance, there is always that one somebody in the workplace who is good at organising the outing; the angel that turns up religiously each week to make the tea and coffee at church; the effective charity fundraiser; the saint who magically brings care and love to the needy. These can all be vocations.

It is worth thinking about and writing something about what your vocation may be. Is it an activity that has been with you a long time? Something that you have always done? It will certainly be something that brings you satisfaction and adds meaning to your life. You may have done it for so long that you have not really given a lot of thought to what it is or to the benefits it brings to you and to others. And remember that vocations are often unpaid. But they are matters that we are good at and that are important to us. Another test of vocation is that they are things that people come to us for. We are well known for these gifts. If you can identify these, can you envisage what role these may have for you in your future journey?

Another simple way to think about what you enjoy and are good at is to undertake a very simple Examen. This is a technique used in Ignatian spirituality. Here is a very simplified version of it, to ask yourself two basic questions. 'What brings me to life?' and 'What deadens me?' Do this by dividing a sheet of paper into two columns and quickly jot down what immediately comes into your head. We'll return to this later, because here is a valuable trigger to prompt your writing.

Discernment

What we are looking at here is how to discern who we really are and where we are heading. We notice in all the work we both do with others – in spiritual accompaniment, coaching, training, retreats and almost all human interaction – the question invariably arises of 'What next?' It is top of their mind for so many, the perennial question.

I (Richard) struggled for many years earlier in life trying to define my essential purpose. I wrote a lot about the subject and always wrestled with whether it was me or God who was saying what I heard or thought I heard. Then I grew to realise that it was the still small voice within me coming through. I didn't need a written heavenly confirmation or a divine thunderbolt. I wasn't getting those anyway.

> My own journey of discernment started in earnest on a five-day silent retreat. It was when I accidentally became a vicar. I had booked onto the retreat at the very last minute and didn't realise it was solely for the ordained. I was therefore given a name badge bearing the title Revd Richard Palmer. It made me feel a bit swanky and feel that I should be a bit more serious over the forthcoming days.
>
> As it was a silent retreat, I couldn't explain to the others that I was just a common and garden lay chap. I did consider a complex charade, miming the ripping off of a dog collar. This would entail some silent barking which I wasn't sure I could pull off, unless I ran around the dinner table on all fours. I decided this might be a tad over the top at one of our communal silent suppers. And to be honest, by day three we had all only just managed to learn the sign language for pass the salt, please. Also, having

Looking forward

> three cooked meals a day we were all a bit podged and gassy and soon learnt the quizzical facial expression one made to indicate 'It wasn't me' when someone had a flatulent interlude, an event that I noted was a lot more noticeable on silent retreats. So, after a week of ordination and flatulence, the vicar pose didn't feel right. I was pleased to return to being a lay person and it helped me to decide that I didn't want to pursue any formal role in the church.

Oh dear! I should have deleted the last two paragraphs. But I use them as an example of you never know where writing will take you. Because when I sat down to write this morning, I had no idea this little vignette, which is true, would emerge from my subconscious. But it did. It really needs deleting but it stays as a real-life example of starting to write and seeing where it takes you! I could have developed this piece to talk about silence and how revealing it is. Or how it was strange that in the absence of speech, we all were growing to know one another quite well as we sat together in silence for five days.

Back to the retreat, I took with me Gerard W. Hughes' seminal book, *God of Surprises*. And it was a huge surprise, a turning point for me in my journey. It triggered many things in me and I started in earnest to write and journal a lot at this stage. I started to read more about discernment and looked at different ways to discern.

My key discernment tool was writing. It was a tremendous help in sorting the fact from the fiction and in doing a brain dump of all that was flowing through my mind. A lot of the writing was messy. These were not neatly-formed notes on the meaning of life but sometimes splurges of feeling, spurts of anger, and so forth.

I also experimented with pushing doors as part of this discernment process and wrote down the outcomes over time. Some doors unexpectedly slammed in my face. This surprised me since they were good, well-developed ideas. But through writing and reflection, I grew to realise that the timing of these ideas was premature, plus I gave them to the to the wrong people who had too many of their own personal agendas to take notice. An interesting conundrum.

But other doors gave way very easily and led to further unexpected doors opening. Upon reflection, this was because I dealt with positive and open-minded people, who did not impose their own hidden agendas. I learnt to avoid the *Yes-But* people and went with the *Yes-And* folk. You might like to write a short piece on the people you know who fit in to these two categories, *The Yes-Buts* versus *The Yes-Ands*.

I took a longer-term view with some of the ideas that came to me and planted seeds and watered them conscientiously with thought and care to see what transpired. Eventually some grew well and matured. This book has come from those roots.

I studied and read a lot. Also, I talked to more folks about what my dreams were. I collected people's views and wrote them down. I collected words of encouragement and gratitude from people. This told me much about myself, and I became much more aware of what people saw as my strengths. The third-party confirmations are always more welcome and have far more resonance than our own views. Plus, others can see things in us that we do not see. Pay attention to this. We can all learn. Listen to those whom you trust and avoid the naysayers.

I also started a daily walk routine in lockdown which has stayed with me, a great process for reflection. And I paid more attention to what I see in nature and in art, all wonderful sources of inspiration for our writing and discernment.

Looking forward

> And never forget your instincts. They advise you from a deep place. They are there to keep you safe and protect you. Don't ignore them, If it doesn't feel right, it most probably isn't.
>
> In today's world of scientific supremacy, artificial intelligence and technological advancement, it becomes easy to overrule our own instinctive feelings and also to dismiss the mystery and unknowing inherent in our own spiritual journey.

And I then daydreamed.

Daydreaming

I've called it daydreaming. To be honest, it covers any form of silence, listening to the beat of your life, the rhythm of your heart, the circling of the cosmos, the still small voice of God.

You can meditate, contemplate, pray, be mindful, go on a retreat, take a quiet meditative walk, do tai chi, yoga (put that thesaurus down) or whatever floats your boat. The important point is to take your mind out of gear, as you would when you put your car into neutral. Be disengaged. Let your mind bathe and refresh itself. If you find difficulty zoning out, a repetitive prayer or mantra can help to still your mind. After the busy monkey mind has subsided, you may start to gain a sense of peace and tranquillity. You may be well versed in one of these techniques. If you are not, try daydreaming. A warm, comfortable, quiet space is all that is required.

The plus point of daydreaming is that we all know how to do it and can start immediately with no training or manual. It is that wonderful feeling that we had as children, falling asleep and dreaming of magic and wonder. Let this happen and you can often sense new thoughts and

The Art of Spiritual Writing

ideas emerging. Warm baths and spa days are also good lubricants.

Our minds like to sort things out. All that writing, the notes, the journal. It is all captured material. New combinations of ideas may arise. In doing this, we are giving ourselves permission to be creative. You are no longer steering your mind towards the daily chores, the do-list, the insurance renewal and the shopping.

Stay with this meditative state. It does not matter if you fall asleep. That may be a part of the refreshment. But, top tip, don't fall asleep when out walking or on the train or you will end up stepping into the canal or missing your station.

And of course as already discussed, keep a notebook by you on these occasions. Note any particular feelings, revelations, ideas, words, lines of dialogue, or whatever comes to you. These dreamlike thoughts and ideas come from special deep places. Such ideas can often engender spiritual writing at its best.

> *You never have to change anything you got up in the middle of the night to write.*
> Saul Bellow

If this all sounds a bit airy-fairy, that is because it is. As W. Somerset Maugham once quipped, 'There are three rules for writing a novel. Unfortunately, no one knows what they are.' There is so much truth therein. The creative muse is an untamed spirit and you have to give it the time and space to play and create and deliver to you the seeds for your writing. You can then grow these on, nurturing them until they are ripe for harvest. After harvesting this crop, your role as a writer is to turn these raw ingredients through the process of writing, rewriting, editing and refining until it is something that is digestible, delectable and nourishing for the reader.

That all sounds simple. But if you can achieve this, just in small ways to start with, you will have discovered something of the art of spiritual writing and the gifts and rewards of turning your inner thoughts into the written word.

This is me

Which pair of wings will you use to fly forward? Where do you want to go to? There is a whole basket of things to consider. Your hopes and fears, your strengths and weaknesses. There is much that can hold you back and writing about those can be cathartic. But do concentrate on the positives. As Pope John XXIII said in his quote at the start of this chapter, 'Concern yourself not with what you tried and failed but with what it is still possible for you to do.' Here is the subject matter to write about now.

Frederick Buechner nailed this when he said, 'The place God calls you to is the place where your deep gladness and the world's deep hunger meet.' Great food for a thoughtful piece of writing!

True self

You can take this further and deeper by thinking on your true self. True self is who we really are. As we grow older, we become more conscious of this self, as opposed to that false self that we needed earlier in life to stamp out our early identity, to finish our education, find a partner, get a job, have kids, make a nest, or whatever lifestyle we chose to follow.

True self. This is the destination for which we can aim as we progress in our spiritual writing, the land where we can explore those heart-words of forgiveness, tolerance, gratefulness, understanding, humility, simplicity and love. These are the words to write about now. This is less about soul-searching, but more about searching for our soul. We are in the good company of the poet, the priest and the philosopher. Here is the land of symbolism, mystery and metaphor, imagery and story, angels and devils, a place where your writing can really come into its own.

Past, present and future

The journey we are on in our writing is the transition from roots to wings, from the past, through the present, to the future. At this juncture of writing this book, our new grandson is just 10 days old. He is at the very beginning of his journey. It is sobering to think that he doesn't have much of a past yet. We as the writers and you, as the readers, have much history to draw upon and much we can examine and write about of our past, of our present times and of looking forward.

Writing about our future journey is very different from writing about our past and present. The past is very much like a film. It has all been recorded. It is all captured in your mind. Some of it is a bit tarnished and it can take a bit of time finding the right reel. But it's there somewhere, as a cherished memory or as an event that happened and affected you. And you have the original, the *director's cut*. No one else has seen the full film. We let others see an edited version, omitting some elements and enhancing the importance of other parts. As far as your spiritual writing is concerned, it is best to get down the *director's cut*, the full story. You can then edit out those parts you wish to remain private. But the 'full monty' is what you are after in your first draft.

The present is an easier gig. It's life at the moment and occupies the majority of our thinking time. We've discussed the status quo situation in the chapter on present times – who we are, identity and current circumstances. There is also the daily round, the insistent ongoing dialogue going on with self. It is dynamic. All those daily anxieties and decisions, choices to make, planning and organising, issues with other people, sorting and shifting. By tomorrow, many of today's concerns are already part of your past. The niggly ones stick around to haunt you or tap you on

Looking forward

the shoulder at 3 a.m. with a sharp 'Oi!' to remind you that you still haven't sorted them. Spiritual writing can help here. Write them down honestly and openly. Putting a problem, concern or issue in writing can often help ameliorate the situation. By articulating, on the page, some of the sting subsides, solutions and healing can result. We talk later about how freewriting or daily pages can help with these.

As we say, the future journey is different. To use the film analogy, our writing about the future is the film script of the film we'd now like to make. There are lots of givens to help us on the way. Many of the cast are already chosen. Location is known. The scene has been set and you, the only viewer at this time may have some ideas you'd like to include. Start to explore these on the page. Consulting with other players on this will be important once your ideas are down in writing. This is an incremental process, proceeding from that urgent and heartfelt first draft to a finely polished well-informed script. And this is what we do instinctively at those key decision moments, those big life changes like going to college, finding a new job, moving home, starting a family.

> Now writing the future for me (Eirene) at one time would feel impossible. Or, like a piece of Physics homework at my grammar school, something which I just had to do whether I could or not. It would have felt a petrifying task in my already stressful day. I never understood Physics although Brian Cox makes things a lot clearer for me now than ancient Mr Sharp back in the days of One Alpha.
>
> And writing the future felt impossible when I was young because I grew up expecting at any moment the Four Horsemen of the Apocalypse would come riding down our street whilst I was watching *Blue Peter*. Although I expect Valerie Singleton might have done something creative

with four plastic Fairy Liquid bottles and a couple of toilet roll tubes to herald their arrival.

But I was a worrier you see, and for worriers, the future, being by definition, unknown, will always feel scary. I've been a worrier long before it was okay to talk about it. In these days of everyone emoting, including our previously buttoned-up Royals, it's inconceivable to remember that at one time, it was just not done to admit to struggling with feelings. You gritted your teeth, hitched up your big-girl pants and put the kettle on.

But with the God I know now, the one who knows me with all my fractures and failings and fears, it's feeling, shall we say, safer to imagine the future. And to write it. And I think in the future I want to write about three things. Faith, hope and love. (Thanks St Paul.)

I reckon we all need hope right now. And for me, holding onto the fact of hope also means holding on to the conviction that somehow, somewhere in all the fear and panic and distress and hurt and chaos of the world, there is a loving Creator who wants to see us through it. And if I believe that, then I also believe that I can talk to her and ask for her help. The Third Order of Franciscans say they recognise the 'power of intercessory prayer' and I reckon the state of God's world is keeping quite a few of them on their knees at the moment.

What does hope look like? It looks a lot like love. It's the kid who has her arm around the kid who's not picked for the team. It's stopping to buy a hot chocolate and a BLT for the guy sleeping in the doorway. It's rocking up to pack bags at the foodbank because you said you would. It's schlepping into town on bitterly cold January night to make sandwiches for the night shelter.

Looking forward

It's making a coffee for the window cleaner on a freezing day. It's all about love.

So for me, writing the future means writing about hope and love. Hope and love which are rooted in something – someone bigger than ourselves. Bigger than all this – the violence, the sorrow, the darned injustices and terror beamed daily into our sitting rooms on the news every night. You could call it faith.

Faith, hope and love.

When I was young, I didn't understand what faith looked like. I went to church because I didn't have anywhere else to go on Sundays. Now, there is part of me that still doesn't have anywhere else to go on Sundays. Like Doubting Thomas I long for the reassurance of an arm around my shoulders, a comforting hug, my hand in his side. I receive these things in the safe space of my church. It's almost as though I have lived a life of two halves – the top half with its carapace of disbelief, the soft underneath of yearning, of vulnerability, of reaching out to hope and love. This is the part that dons cassock and surplice and sings. This is the part that drowns in the most exquisite words and harmonies and instead of encountering oblivion, finds itself more alive than it has ever felt before. This is where my stone is rolled away, where I emerge from the tomb, blinking in the sunlight to encounter resurrection, my road to Emmaus when I realise who was there all the time.

This is a bigger God who embraces me. One who understands hollowness and emptiness. One who knows that the grief of separation can almost annihilate and no amount of cosy chat about prepared mansions will change anything. One who doesn't provide answers but allows me to find my own. And never rejects anyone for

> believing something different. A trusted priest-friend of mine tells me that there is a verse in Mark 11:22 where Jesus tells his disciples to 'have faith in God'. This, she says has been interpreted widely down the centuries as something that we have to do, whereas the original Greek reads more as an invitation for us to hold onto the faithfulness of God. It is something God does. We just hold on. And through all those years when I didn't feel anything, any connection, any sense of belonging, any relationship because I simply could not subscribe to the version of God I was fed, I think now that I was holding onto someone, somewhere, somehow, in the darkness. Maybe that was faith.
>
> So in writing the future, I need to write about these three things, faith, hope and love. And I will encounter my expansive, loving, generous and spacious God. Who holds onto me.

Yes, it is dreaming and discerning, wishing and hoping, praying and planning. It's not new. It's what many of us spend our time doing in those idle moments and those liminal times before and after sleep. We do it because it is exciting, engaging, dynamic and brings us hope and solace for the future. The key difference and the essence of this book is to write them down to assist your own processes of discernment.

Once again, the map below is a summary, showing some elements covered in this chapter that can help us to reflect about the future of our spiritual journey. Use it as a snapshot to see what ideas for writing it brings to mind. And there are four writing prompts that pick up other themes covered.

That completes our examination of the spiritual journey for now. We shall look in the next chapter at the

Looking forward

benefits of freewriting with Eirene before we go on to review the creative ways of developing our own style of spiritual journalling with Richard.

FROM ROOTS TO WINGS
From the past. Through the present. To the future.

Spiritual journey
THE FUTURE

MY WINGS

- Instincts
- Hopes and fears
- Vocation
- What others come to me for
- Accepting mystery
- Finding true self
- Dreams

DISCERNMENT

- Writing
- Journalling
- Day dreaming
- Prayer, meditation
- Pushing doors
- Talking with others
- The Examen

What are your dreams? Write about them.....

Writing prompts

The Examen
Take the list we suggested earlier containing the two columns of 'What brings me to life?' and 'What deadens me?' Pick a favourite item that brings life to you and write about the last time you undertook this, what really makes you like it, your plans on how to use or do this in future. Whatever aspect of it that brings you to life is worthy of exploration. It may lead you to consider associated activities.

Did you list a pet hate? Write about it and get it off your chest.

Daydreaming
Do it. It's all discussed above. No rules, just a comfortable warm space, free of interruption. Wallow in the freedom of time and space for yourself. Don't set a time and get into the habit of doing it whilst you progress through this book.

Scriptwriting
Are there any key scenes that you would like to see in your next film of your life? Spend some time considering these video clips. If you thought about the recap sequence earlier on, you can play this in your mind before you come up with ideas for the way forward. Choose one scene and write about it.

SWOT
SWOT is a planning tool commonly used to analyse a situation, project, plan or problem. It can also be used to think about your own self. Have you ever considered your

Looking forward

own Strengths and Weaknesses, your Opportunities and Threats? Write a couple of paragraphs on each of these headings. When complete, concentrate on the positive aspects of this and how you could engage with your strengths and potential opportunities.

CHAPTER 5
Freewriting

I write entirely to find out what I'm thinking, what I'm looking at, what I see and what it means. What I want and what I fear.

Joan Didion

Freewriting. What is it? The first phrase which pops into my sluggish brain is 'writing freely'. Ah yes. And I (Eirene) thought I was struggling with this.

When I was in junior school, we were given an insipid green exercise book with the name of the local education authority stamped on the cover, told to write our name and class on the front and call it 'Freewriting.' Freewriting we were told meant we could write just what we liked. We could write a composition that could be about anything at all. I was delighted.

However, my first efforts were somewhat laboured. '*I went to my nana's house for dinner last satday (sic). I had chips and kidney and cup of gravy.*' The gravy was obviously important and worthy of a mention. Another entry details my early artistic efforts. '*Painted picture called solitude after dinner – two trees, sky, ground.*' Later I graduated to making things up. '*One day I caught a buglar. (sic). I rushed forward and tried to get the man but he ran away.*'

Now I have no recollection in my early days of being a mini-vigilante but I obviously harboured a desire to perform my civic duty and catch a burglar (or even a buglar). This

Freewriting

story extends over several pages and eventually climaxes with my making a citizen's arrest, '*I rushed forward and got him.*' (There I go, rushing again). I was learning the art of imagination.

I was writing what I wanted to write about instead of having to describe a porcupine or the fight between Beowulf and Grendel.

It took me a long, long time to realise that writing what you wanted to write about could involve feelings. People didn't have feelings so much in the Sixties, and if they did, they squashed them down because it was a bit shameful to wear them on the outside. No one wanted to know if you felt unaccountably sad when the cat died. Or even when your grandma died. Things have changed now, and for the better.

A light switched on in my head when I realised that writing what I wanted to write about instead of conforming to someone else's agenda could set me free. Free writing sets you free. That puts me in mind of that glorious verse in John 8:32, 'the truth will set you free'. For me, writing my truth set me free.

Now this idea isn't rocket science despite the millions of words which have been written about it. It means – just write. Just tumble the words onto the page without thinking about punctuation, grammar, or spelling. If there are any little nuggets to save for later – you'll know. Don't let them hold you up. Some find it helpful to set a timer and scribble or tap until it goes off. The timer can be set at five, fifteen, twenty minutes – whatever you like. Then just go. Put down your thoughts without fretting over structure or form or appropriateness or any of the zillion and one niggles which beset a writer's life as they dare to make marks on the page. At the risk of sounding like a Seventies charismatic chorus writer – 'Let it flow'.

Daily Pages

But just to prove this isn't me making things up (though isn't that what we writers do?), here are three people who have written about this very thing. And written successfully, enough to dine out on their ideas for some considerable dinner party invitations.

The first is Julia Cameron. You can't go very far in a creative writing class without coming across the idea of Julia Cameron and her 'Morning Pages.' If you Google 'Morning Pages' you will be furnished with hundreds of references to Cameron's *The Artists Way*, a book that has changed the creative landscape for many. She rightly deserves the accolades heaped upon her. She describes Morning Pages as 'three pages of longhand, stream of consciousness writing done first thing in the morning'.

The concept of writing pages first thing in the morning was recommended sixty years earlier by Dorothea Brande in her book, *Becoming a Writer* which just goes to show that even in the age of the typewriter, writers were looking for different and inspirational ways of harnessing their thoughts and emotions. Brande says, 'Write anything that comes into your head: last night's dream, if you are able to remember it; the activities of the day before; a conversation, real or imaginary; an examination of conscience.'

And she goes on, 'The rewards – you will see that our "morning's pages" are fuller and better than before. It is not only that you are bringing new material to them every day, but you are stirring the latent memories in your mind.'

Other writers have picked up this ball and run with it. Gillie Bolton in her book, *The Writer's Key* suggests that writing freely for just six minutes every day is enough to make a big difference. She notes, 'It is key of keys to the mansion of creative expression and explorative writing.'

They are all talking about the same thing. Writing freely every day. Julia Cameron advocates three pages of longhand at roughly 750 words. Dorothea Brande preferred

Freewriting

her typewriter. Gillie Bolton suggests whatever feels good to you. One isn't right and the all the others wrong. It really is whatever works for you.

They all advocate a time and space where you will be comfortable and uninterrupted. And the challenge is to write without stopping. Let the words come. Do away with the censor niggling away on your shoulder telling you that you can't say that. You can. You can say anything.

And all tell you not to bother with niceties such as punctuation, spelling, and grammar. You may have sat in Miss Moldoff's Eng Lang class for long dreary years in your hormone bustin' teens – but she's not around now and she's not going to tell you off and mark you down. And if you do happen to bump into her years later in the garden centre (happened to me), you just don't mention morning pages. (Although she might be doing them herself now.)

In our house, it's my husband who is the Morning Pages buff. He really goes for it and has written his way through several crises over the years. Over half a million words in two years.

Now we are writing this book together and it's taking us some considerable time. Not only writing time, but talking time, planning time, and peering into our half-empty glasses in the pub time. And we are aiming for a combined word count of say 45-50,000. But each word has to count and earn its place. It can't just hang out pretending to fit in with all the others. It has to mean something. It has be spellchecked, have all its ducks in a row as far as punctuation and grammar are concerned and make a difference. Morning Pages are not like that. Quantity over quality is perfectly acceptable – if not required. That's the difference.

You get the drift. And if you want much more erudite information on all these authors then pick up one of the books I've mentioned. They are all listed in *Signposts* at the end of the book. Go for it. And write what you really want to write about. Really. You're not in Class 1 now having to include all the details of the set topic of the day. No one is going to mark it, censor it or tell your family. You can even write about them if you like.

The Monkey Pen

The Buddhists have a principle called the 'monkey mind.' It refers to the notion of the mind leaping about like a monkey, jumping from tree to tree, branch to branch, constantly on the move and unable to settle. Think of a David Attenborough documentary (unless you are much well-travelled and have seen the antics of the jungle for yourself). We all have a 'monkey mind' at some point, even the most chilled-out dude who appears so laid back as to be almost asleep. No one is immune from restlessness, agitation, or confusion.

Picking up a pen can feel like this. We call it the 'Monkey Pen'. For a writer it can be a source of release and inspiration to let the pen jump over the page. Let it land where it will. Let it wander, explore, go down a blind alley, chase after a choice morsel, sometimes striking lucky, sometimes not. Let your inner monkey pen roam.

One thing that this will do – all of it – any of it, is give you access to your subconscious or unconscious mind. This can sound scary, but it's all part of you and it can be as well to make friends with the bits of you you can't see. It can be another source of ideas, an open door which seemed so firmly shut tight. It can enable healing of that monkey mind. It can also be a ticket to that imagination of yours which would like free rein sometimes and just needs permission to roam free. Writers all down the years have employed this technique. It even has a name these days – the 'stream of consciousness'. Think of your conscious mind, running like a river, never stopping, embracing everything in its path, the good, the bad, the shameful, the jubilant, the heroic, the connections with people past, present and those you are yet to meet. There are many famous examples of this genre of stream of consciousness writing, but here is a less famous one by Richard.

Freewriting

It's difficult to know sometimes, isn't it everyone says that but then we all pretend we know
what's right - that we do know I'm very dubious what I heard yesterday but some folks are
consummate tellers of untruths **Fib-lets, mini-fibs are possibly ok** I like the word fiblet
think we invented it we all do the fiblet thing occasionally but the real whopping lies should
be illegal the web is killing the truth – whopping or whooping
That dream I had where was truth in that the forest with the floor covered in lovely
buoyant flowers. then the stinking river I noticed in the distance that spoilt it all scary it smelt
brown should have been gin-clear with fish in was that last night or the night before can't remember
but we've got to get a move on move with all these damned bits that keep getting in the way
of everything like there's debris all over the path no not path but the journey and you
can't get moving until you've cleared it swept off the path because you'll get a puncture and
that will delay you still further Are we on bikes why does my spellcheck say tincture
for puncture, but actually that's interesting, another way of looking at the journey, needing a
salve to heal or **a salve to solve** that's a good title I like that – pun-like
it's already Wed and it should still be Mon morn because I've got nothing finished salve to solve try it on for size
I'm trying to find a salve to rub into my issues and solve them says on the tube use up to three times a day and apply liberally to larger problems

The Art of Spiritual Writing

> not suitable for children under five who are great problem solvers anyway
>
> Perhaps as adults we worry far too much about probs we have just slap on some salve and get on with life

Thanks. (It's okay, you're back with me [Eirene] now.) This is exactly the kind of writing we're talking about. No punctuation. No sentences. No correct grammar. Just all the contents of his mind, churning and churning and out onto the page describing the details of his day.

Above all, let your monkey pen words stand up for you.

> Big words, little words, long words, short words, colourful words, all shades of grey words, emotive, tedious, transforming, defiant, revolutionary, provocative words. It's words I need. Words help me express silence and give me a voice. Beyond everything else, words give me a voice.
>
> Words are powerful. Words can wound as well as comfort. Words can explain, spell it out, describe, tell a story, tell truth. Words can illuminate all the shadows.
>
> Find your own voice and use it. Find your own words. Words are your friends. Words stand up for you. They are there in their thousands, millions, all lined up in serried ranks like soldiers, waiting to take up their rifles and fire volley after volley in your defence.
>
> I can never have too many words. I can battle insecurities about not being good enough, with words. I can hold words, understand them and emerge if not whole, at least better, through my ability and facility to engage with words. I need to give them flesh and life, bones and blood, a

> heartbeat, energy, and power. I need to set them free from their two-dimensional life on a page of A4 and allow them to go where they will. I need to feel vindicated, liberated. I need to be released.
>
> I need my chains to fall off and my heart to be free. And for that, I need to write words.

So pick up your monkey pen and write!

That first draft

We've all been there. We've all sat down at our desk or at our table, pen in hand, keyboard waiting and known we have an IDEA. It may have come as the result of all those daily pages we've written. We may have mined for gold and found a nugget. And now we want to write the best thing we have ever written. It might even be a bestseller.

> *I'm writing a first draft and reminding myself that I'm simply shovelling sand into a box so that later, I can build castles.*
>
> Shannon Hale

But before any of that can happen, we have to write a first draft. And this is where reality kicks in. That first draft is highly unlikely to bring us fame and fortune or even a deal of satisfaction. It's getting words down onto the page. Just getting the words down so there is something there. This is where freewriting comes in. This is where the hours, days, weeks you have put into familiarity with your craft pays off. This is where allowing access to your unconscious thoughts, making yourself open and available bear fruit. You become vulnerable not victim. It all shows in that first draft.

The Art of Spiritual Writing

> *Get it down. Take chances. It may be bad, but it's the only way you can do anything really good.*
> William Faulkner

Faulkner won the Nobel Prize for Literature in 1949 so he must have written a fair few bad drafts in his time. Every successful writer has. John McPhee, a journalist who has written extensively for *Time* magazine and the *New Yorker* and is considered to be one of the pioneers of modern creative non-fiction wrote, 'Sometimes in a nervous frenzy I just fling words as if I were flinging mud at a wall. Blurt out, heave out, babble out something — anything — as a first draft…Until it exists, writing has not really begun.'

This is freewriting. This is what we've been talking about. Close the door and write. Here's how I do my first draft.

> I sit at my desk, open my laptop, and begin my diversionary tactics.
>
> I know these little blighters are coming so I'm gentle with them. Check emails, check Facebook, check WhatsApp to see if any cute pictures of grandchildren have been posted overnight, check Instagram to see where in the world my itinerant musician daughter is today, make more coffee, check the weather, decide to write.
>
> As Anne Lamott says in *Bird by Bird*, 'You try to sit down at approximately the same time every day. This is how you train your unconscious to kick in for you creatively.'
>
> At first it is tortuous. I can't write, I've never written anything worthwhile in my life. I am fooling myself. I am a charlatan, an imposter, a fraud. I should just go and eat worms. But gradually the words begin to come and when they do, I relax

Freewriting

a little and lose myself and the fears of being phoney reduce and recede and I find myself again. I am connected and I am happy.

I look up and two hours have passed. I make more coffee and set off again. Eventually all the other demands and insistences of the day begin to crowd in and I and realise that the morning has gone.

And afterwards …

I go over the road to the leisure centre to swim and as I swim, I process all my sub-conscious has dictated to me this morning. It's a kind of cleansing in the waters. I need this ritual to shake off the bogeys and long-leggedy beasties and surface with a clean and clearer mind.

The afternoons are filled with domesticity, with caring for my 97-year-old mum who is childlike in her need for love, for reassurance, for predictability. And having six adult kids means someone is always wanting to talk about child-rearing, applying for a new job, needing the recipe for salmon pasta or alerting me to the news that our five-year-old granddaughter has finally stopped vomiting. Later in the day, if I can, I return to my study and look at what I have written.

Maybe some of it will do, I think.

Beachcombing

Every year, when I was a kid, we went to the seaside in the summer. Coming from a city known as 'The Furthest from The Sea', this was a huge event in my young life and one greatly anticipated from around the middle of January. I have many fond memories of scrabbling around in the sand finding 'treasure' which I would wrap carefully in my dad's handkerchief and transport the hundred and twenty miles back home on the train. This little collection of shells, pebbles, seaweed (could smell rancid after a while) sat on the window shelf in my bedroom and brought me infinite delight. It talked to me of an alternative universe, one on which I could play on the beach every day, paddling, building sandcastles, digging trenches. Beachcombing – finding your own treasure in the vast expanse of sea and sand.

Find your own nuggets of gold on your beach of words, and use them. Trust me, they will be there. Record them in a Word document or in a notebook. Come back to them frequently. Some words you will be dying to use because they are just so flippin' good. But not yet. Not until the time is right. You can't rush these things. And above all, 'kill your darlings'. This is a phrase writers use to compel themselves to only use those words which are necessary. You may have written the most erudite, sparkling phrase known to man, but if it doesn't fit – don't use it.

And I've said it so many times, but I'll say it again. It's all about giving yourself permission to write your-self. It's all about finding your own authentic voice.

And that is where a journal can be so fruitful, too. Richard will talk about this in the next chapter.

Writing prompts

Clock watching
Close the door. Set out your pen and notebook or fire up your laptop. Set a timer for five, six, ten minutes – however long you like. Pick up your pen or your mouse. Then write until the timer goes off. Write without thinking, without hesitation, without censoring. Just Write.

Take two ideas

Take two ideas or words or thoughts from that session and write a first draft of a story or a piece of prose or a poem. It's not going to be perfect. 'The worst thing you write is better than the best thing you didn't write' (Anon).

CHAPTER 6
Spiritual Journalling

'Keeping a journal,' says John Sanford, 'is the most inexpensive form of psychotherapy I know ... A journal is a book in which we record all matters of importance for our conscious life. We write down our dreams, our fantasies, our urges and our creative thoughts. In our journal, we write down our problems, what is worrying us, what is getting us down and our darkest most unthinkable thoughts. Anything of importance to the life of the soul can be written in our journal.'
From *Keeping a Spiritual Journal*, Edward England (editor)

Everyone's at it! Journalling has come of age. A quick Google search reveals so many forms of journalling that it becomes bewildering – self-care, gratitude, kids' journals, women's journals, art, daily reflection, dreams, goals and planning, men's journals, pet loss journals. What? Pet loss? Yes. And why not. It can be a traumatic event for many of us. We were extremely shaken when our notoriously naughty terrier went to doggy heaven (we believe in a gracious God), despite the angst that his special-needs behaviour had caused us.

The journal list goes on. Ad infinitum. All are valid for the right person at the right time. And all are valuable as they engage the individual in writing down their thoughts, dreams, aspirations and much more.

Spiritual Journalling

Journalling has put on a new fashionable set of clothes but it is not a new phenomenon. It is a long-established tried and tested formula for understanding more of ourselves. No matter how you carve up the classifications of journalling, it comes down to recording and understanding our self, our life and self-improvement. And it can stretch across a lifetime, starting with all that angsty poetry of adolescence, right through to reflective reminiscences in older age.

Journalling is a very personal thing. And because it is personal, it is important to do what is right for you in your journalling. Just as we develop our own handwriting in life, it is most likely that you will do similarly with your journal. There are no *'thou shalts'* in journalling. Instead, what follows is lots of general advice on the art and craft of journalling.

Journeying and Journalling

Underpinning all of the journalling experience is the strong connection with journeying. Again, a sudden interest has bloomed in the word *journey* but that doesn't undermine the importance of it.

We call this connection the Two J's – Journeying and Journalling. Whatever your journal is about, it will eventually lead you back to your journey. You write in your journal about your journey. What you write in your journal can affect your journey. It influences the decisions you make and the conclusions you reach. And these then affect your forward journey. It is a symbiotic relationship.

This symbiotic relationship between your journey and your journal leads you straight towards the goal of developing your spiritual writing. Here's a little equation that sets out the relationship.

The equation

We start with the idea of our journey. Let's call it your life's journey. Both of us in our former lives did a lot of interviewing and thousands of CVs passed through our hands.

The Art of Spiritual Writing

Sometimes these were terribly-written pieces of work, but more often than not they were carefully-crafted, highly-polished stories of work careers. Sometimes they were so sanitised and full of self-congratulatory aggrandisement that you thought this was the Angel Gabriel, sent down from heaven to undertake some first-hand earthly work experience.

In fairness most CVs were fairly accurate, yet *clean-cut* life stories. But we all know life is not all roses and boxes of chocolates. That's the difference between the life journey and the spiritual journey. The latter has all the cuts and grazes, the laughter and tears, and the joys and sorrows of life included. It contains the truth that you don't wish to publicise in your job applications. These are the truths that only you know about. And that is where the journal comes in.

Is a journal a diary? What's the difference? For the purposes of this book, diaries are fairly factual observations on the day – diary dates, weather, visitors, appointments, reminders and so forth. This is a bit like the sanitised CV. We're not giving much away in the diary. It is often just factual stuff. No feelings please! Some may start to introduce opinions and thoughts, feelings and emotions. Then it starts to become more like a journal.

A journal is far more about your personal journey. It is the births, marriages and deaths pages of your life, highs, lows and hollow middles. Why was Erica such a bitch towards me today? Where was God in that accident yesterday? My boss just doesn't understand me! What a great day with the family! Oh God, where are you in all this terrible mess I'm in - is prayer the only answer? Anguish, delight, unknowing, mystery, problems. Then your journal starts to become a spiritual journal and your writing takes on its own depth.

An equation is starting to form. Considering our life's journey as our *spiritual journey* and our journalling as our *spiritual journal* we arrive at:

Spiritual Journalling

Spiritual Journey + Spiritual Journal

We are close to solving the equation. We've talked of the sanitised CV reflecting only part of the life journey and how the inclusion of the whole life story, warts and all, becomes the authentic journey, that is, the spiritual journey.

And we are not going to just write down details in a straightforward diary. We are going to write about all the helter-skelter of life and the big dipper ride in our spiritual journal. And that step from diarising to journalling encourages us, as we've said, to write with depth, openness and honesty. And in so doing, this becomes our spiritual writing.

Spiritual Journey + Spiritual Journal = Spiritual Writing

Et voilà. You don't need to solve this or get smart about it. It's not $E=mc^2$ (And incidentally, there are no more equations and no maths tests in this book. Promise.) It just sets out an understanding of the relationship of how thinking of life in spiritual terms and recording it openly and honestly (aka spiritually) leads you towards your spiritual writing and finding your authentic voice.

Safe Space

One key point to make clear is that your journal is a safe space to say what you think about anything or anyone. It is private and confidential, not for sharing. Keep it to yourself if you want it to be totally uncensored. We said that there are no '*thou shalts*' in journalling. But there is one '*it might be really good if thou didst*'. Uncensored is so important. That is what we are after, the raw, deep material. Once the raw material is out on the page you can revise it, stir in some sugar and take out all of those libellous comments you made if you want to share it with others. The important thing is that you have captured in that magical journalling moment what you really feel, the truth of the matter. This can be extremely cathartic. And the material you have produced may trigger a profound piece of writing. The point is a simple but fundamental one. You are granted permission to say what you want in your journal.

The notion of writing privately is an interesting one. Stephen King in his book, *On Writing, a memoir of the craft*, recounts how he writes his first draft of the book with his door closed. It is for him only. Later, when he is ready to do his second draft, he writes with the door open. A small but a very significant symbolic action.

> Journalling is so powerful. We call it the Heineken of writing, because *'journalling reaches the parts that other writing cannot reach'*. It's that simple.

We will concentrate upon one type of journal, the spiritual journal, although many of the principles can be related to other sorts of journal. We'll also reference one other important journal, the Writing Repository. Not a journal per se, but a key part of a writer's tool bag.

The spiritual journal

The emphasis of a spiritual journal can vary tremendously from one person to another. And it can also vary from one time to another, depending upon where we are in our spiritual journey. You may gush with words for a few weeks and then not visit again for a month. You can write every day, or just weekly or sporadically. It is more about when the time is right for you and when the subject matter presents itself.

The nub of the journal is a place for personal reflection, of whatever nature. The safe space enables us to take an honest and open approach to this. Try to get the real you on to the page. The internal censor will be tapping you on the shoulder saying, 'You can't say that!' Well, you can.

Spiritual Journalling

You have permission to vent and curse, bitch and moan, cry, laugh and shout. Just get it out and on to the page. Someone once said, 'Write as if your parents are no longer alive.' It is good advice if your journal is really going to speak to you. Expressing your thoughts and emotions can be most liberating. As an example of the cathartic effect of writing, I cite an example from my work days. At the end of a fraught day, when tired and desolate from the hectic grinding rigours of work, when the last straw has been an angry or very unreasonable email, I would sometimes write quite an acerbic reply to that message. It made me feel so much better. The double six was that I didn't send it. The next morning, bolstered and refreshed, I would delete it from my Drafts file. The top tip was not to put their email address on the reply when I wrote it, then I couldn't send it in error.

Airing a problem in your journal is likewise often helpful. The expression of the problem in writing gives it a concrete nature. Documenting struggles and obstacles is tremendously helpful to give them form. The alternative is to have it swirling around your mind as some amorphous unsolved mess. The solution may not appear immediately. I recall a thorny issue that lasted for several months. To revisit it regularly over time in my journal, I started to see a pattern of unreasonableness in what others were doing and saying and the very clear remedy eventually emerged over time. Sometimes things need the time to brew. As Ruth Fowke says in Edward England's *Keeping a Spiritual Journal*, 'Journalling has proved its use when I have a tough decision to make, when anything is proving to be a particular problem and when I am finding any aspect of a relationship at all unusual.'

Journalling your faith journey

Documenting your faith journey is a big part of many spiritual journals. This can emanate from your daily reflections, your prayer life, matters that speak clearly to you. It can arise when you articulate your convictions, doubts on your faith, when you record the numinous occasions of your walk, when you feel the Universe speak to you, as you express your instinctive thoughts or detect clear occasions of discernment. Journalling can also assist in discerning patterns and rhythms in your walk.

A trip through my journal the other day brought me up sharply. There were several entries from seven years ago, all entries in the space of a couple of weeks. They were typed and stuck in, which meant that they were important to me.

This was at a time when we were making a big change in our lives. There was a bullet point list of things we wanted to pursue. From the list of nine aims, six of them have come to pass. We have never deliberately gone back to check on those aims but through journalling them, they had become a part of our consciousness and our personal drives. This is a shining example of how writing about our present times had a substantial positive effect on our future spiritual journey.

As we read through it together recently, we were both quite amazed how these aims had come about over time. That is one of the powers of journalling, being able to look back and recall where you were and where you are now. Progress and change are often incremental and can be slow. Having a touchstone recorded in your journal showing how you felt at that time and what you wanted to do to change matters can be an excellent way of seeing how far things have moved on.

A part of this journal entry mentioned above was that I had recorded a strong feeling I had about my writing and our writing together. I had an intuitive sense that it was right. I won't reproduce it here because it is quite detailed and I say at the end of several lengthy paragraphs – 'No idea what this is about, I just need to go with it and see what happens. But these are definite thoughts and feelings I have and are the sort of things I'd never share with others. They are just for me. That is quite a good test really that they are not for sharing.'

Very interesting, that I make the comments in my journal that not sharing these thoughts with others was a good test. It was a test of them being numinous, mysterious but really important and personal to me. And in time they came to pass.

Gratitude and learning journalling

Journals are also a good place to note the gratitude that people have given you. Sometimes when your self-confidence is ebbing and you need some self-assurance, to be able to turn to those comments and know what others are grateful for in you, is a real boost. Gratitude journals are a journal in themselves but these can be incorporated into your spiritual journal.

Another potential inclusion in your journal are specific times of learning. Retreats, courses, spiritual events may all have salient matters worth recording, otherwise they fade. Some people keep separate learning journals if they are doing a longer course. Academia loves a bit of self-reflection and these can be very helpful journals if you embark upon a learning journey.

And of course, as already mentioned in the chapter on Looking Forward, the idea of writing down your hopes and aspirations can help enormously in articulating and refining your reflections on your potential future journey.

Creative journalling

When we speak about spiritual journalling on our courses and retreats, we are amazed at how many people are locked into the idea that the journal should be totally words-based. When you consider this, it is not a surprising supposition. This may well arise from the historical context of journalling, which was traditionally an exclusively words-based approach. When we suggest to the group that they can include pictures, doodles and many other visuals, they go away with a spring in their step. It is simply that they have now been granted permission to loosen up their ideas about journalling and they feel quite liberated as a result.

A journal takes on a richness if you can add variety to it, and it also becomes more accessible. Don't feel restricted to just writing a daily log. There are many other sources of material you can use. Consider including anything that speaks to you about your journey, either of your own making or materials from other sources. Your own writing does not have to be all prose. Write a poem, make a list, write a prayer, do a mind map, develop a metaphor for your situation, write in coloured inks. You can be creative with your words.

Incorporate relevant sources from third parties such as favourite prayers, scriptures, articles from papers and magazines, quotes, course materials, passages from books, photocopies or whatever else appears relevant for you. Anything that helps you in your journey, your faith, or your general sense of self is extremely welcome in your journal. It is all good reference material and can be used for generating ideas and articles and stories for your writing later on. Letters can also be good additions and we have talked of these elsewhere.

Your written journal can often be enhanced with the inclusion of graphics. Include such additions if these work for you, such as sketches, doodles, painting, art, cartoons, photographs, icons, postcards, diagrams, cut and paste, scrapbooking, or whatever else takes your fancy. The important thing is to express yourself openly and to find a method of journalling that feels natural to you. That way it won't become a chore.

What goes into your journal is up to you. One personal input I like to include is a mind map of the past year. This is an aide memoir of the year, traditionally done on New Year's Day, or thereabouts. It includes major notable occurrences such as family news, major events attended, holidays, health, travel, the pluses and minuses of the year, written pieces completed, and anything published.

Electronic journalling

You can also keep your journal electronically. This has some advantages. As well as written material, you can easily add graphics, photographs and other materials that can be easily cut and pasted from other online sources. It can become a multisensory journal with the addition of music and videos. This moves further away from the traditional journal. Some will find this appealing, others not. Again, journalling in your own style is important. Whatever works for you.

The writing journal, aka writing repository

You need somewhere to keep your writing. The majority of contemporary writing will be done electronically and can of course be saved in this fashion. But the good pieces, the articles, stories, reminiscences and so forth that really speak to you are worthy of a hard copy. I keep a lever arch file of my favourite work. Somehow, for me, the work seems more real and more easily accessible in a tangible form. Browsing this can also evoke further writing and bring to light earlier work that you may not so easily stumble across on your electronic device.

It is debatable how you divide up different journals. Some will keep their good writing in the spiritual journal. Personally, I find a separate writing file a useful collection of best work. When it is full, I start another. And it can be subdivided as specific themes arise. For example, I keep a specific file on family-related stories. Once again, do what works best for you.

I've already mentioned my maternal grandfather, who was a grocers' assistant. He kept a diary for several years. Two of these diaries survived him, one from 1935 and one from 1941. They were very short entries, two or three sentences per day. My mother typed these up and presented them to our families one Christmas in a loose-leaf file. They were valuable insights, particularly the latter year in wartime, of the privations of war and yet there was a great sense of togetherness and camaraderie in these, a time of going to the pictures, going out dancing, all sorts of social events to keep up peoples' spirits.

But she went further. She included a short family history to colour in the background of the diaries. She also typed up my grandfather's article that appeared in the Stamford Mercury in December 1978, an excerpt of which is included here. Interestingly, what she had in fact done was to produce a mini version of a writing journal of her father's written work. Here is an excerpt of his newspaper article.

> When St Martin's was stirring with life.
>
> When out for a walk, I went to have a look at my old parish of St Martin's in Stamford. I stood at the top of Water Street, and had a touch of nostalgia, and my mind went back to the happy times I had in this part of the town. I was born at No. 1 Phillip's Yard, Water Street in the year 1901, so you can guess I have seen quite a lot of changes during the last 76 years. My word, what a busy and active part of the town it was. It set me thinking of all the things that took place in this parish. ...
>
> ... Coming down Water Street, my, what a busy street. First there was Hunt's brewery and maltings who employed well over 40 men and boys, and brewed a lovely pint of real good ale.
>
> At the old Great Northern station and goods yard, there was even a Smith's bookstall on the platform. It was quite a busy station.
>
> Next, I came to thinking of all the pubs down this street, namely the Fitzwilliam's Arms, the Great Northern Hotel, the Beehive Inn, the Fox and Hounds, the Anchor, and also the Exeter Arms. They brewed their own beer and also had a livery stable. Then Phillip's maltings and brewery and

Spiritual Journalling

the Mineral Water factory, who employed quite a big staff of men and boys. There was also the maltings at the top of the street, and at the corner was J C Cumberland's, who were wine and spirit merchants and also bakers. They had a staff of about 25. I used to work at this shop for over 22 years – and what a busy shop it was.

Further down the street was Hudson's the bakers, and Mrs Bunkey Freeman, Mr Walker the tailor, and Mr Blades the barber. Also, there was a fish and chip shop and Mr Harry Deer's boot shop. It was here that he first started his business – mainly sixpence a week on the bill – so you see Water Street had its fair share of pubs, maltings and shops.

Next my mind went back to the time when Water Street was crowded with children. Coming to Phillip's Yard, there were only four houses but here were over 20 children. I lived in this yard until 1922, when I got married. I was one of a family of ten.

Then came Duncomb's Yard, where there were about 20 children. Taking the next court, which was Lumby's Terrace, now this really was an interesting place. There were about 26 houses and without doubt well over 100 children lived up there. One family alone, Mr Walker the tailor, had 16 children. Needless to say, they had 2 houses and a lot of people had eight to ten children each – so you can see what a large number of children there were in the parish.

Still standing, I'm pleased to say, is the Old Burghley Alms Houses. In my day they used to be for old married couples, and as a lad I used to see all the men going to St Martin's church on Sunday morning in their long Burghley cloaks.

They were joined by twenty 'Blue Boys and Girls'.

The Art of Spiritual Writing

> It was a charity from St Martin's school, and when they left, both boys and girls were given £5 each, which was quite a lot of money in those days. It was to get the boys tools and for the girls to get clothes for when they went out to 'Service'. I think the charity money is still to be had if you live in this parish …

I include this excerpt as a piece of spiritual writing. This article doesn't crackle with sparkling prose. There are repetitions and some jolts in the flow. But it is writing from the heart and my grandfather talks of the nostalgia of it.

There are happy memories as well, of this part of the town, which in its time was an over-populated and impoverished area. It stands in sharp contrast to the Burghley House estate whose park started at the end of this street. In spite of this strong class division, memories are sweet. And he enjoyed a pint, so there's a detailed record of the pubs along the street. He talks a lot about the people and paints a picture of the bustle of the surroundings. Life was tough in those days and yet these are remembered as good times, albeit in hard circumstances.

Again, this serves as an example of the power of spiritual writing and how it can rise up from the past and become alive to succeeding generations. How very lucky to have this short writing journal of my grandfather's, again a piece of writing produced by someone of limited formal education and with no iota of an idea of ever calling himself a writer, but nevertheless, someone who wanted to record his daily life and talk of his past journey.

Experiment and see what form of journal works for you. For example, if you are completing the writing prompts as you progress through this book, a writing journal will serve as a good place to keep them.

And in your spiritual journal, find a way that makes it fun, not a chore. There are lots of creative journalling ideas on-line. Borrow any ideas that appeal to you. All are valid. We are big fans of encouraging colour, graphics, illustrations, photographs and so on into your written work if that works for you. They enhance rather than detract. Take a lesson from the colour magazines around us.

And don't be surprised if you branch out into other more specific journals as you continue your journalling. It's all fair game in the process of spiritual writing.

The following three chapters identify more ideas that you may like to make a part of your spiritual journalling and your spiritual writing. Eirene leads on the first two of these, *Writing as Therapy,* and *Writing as Prayer.* Richard leads on the third, *The Marvellous Metaphor.*

Writing prompts

New world order
The Coronavirus epidemic and lockdown caused seismic changes in society throughout the world. These will be well documented in history. But what happened for you? Write something on what changed for you personally as a result of COVID. Include your feelings. Remember that we did not know how or when this would end and if, indeed, we would survive. Write it for a succeeding generation to read.

Strongest memory
My strongest memory this year: if you were writing your own obituary, what event, feeling or thought would you include from this year?

The Art of Spiritual Writing

Pen picture
Recall where you grew up. Paint a picture so that readers can glean the nature and culture of your upbringing. Start with a target of 1000 words.

Creative journalling
Take time to look on-line to see how others approach creative journalling and try one new idea in your journal.

CHAPTER 7
Writing as therapy

I can shake off everything as I write; my sorrows disappear, my courage is reborn.

Anne Frank

'Don't you think it's rather self-indulgent?' he asks.

Now I (Eirene) like to think of myself as a good person. (Don't we all.) I like to think of myself as the decent sort who would take a stray puppy to the vet and pay for all its injections, or help an infirm aged lady across the road on a bitter snowy day. (I tried this once, noting she was struggling with a heavy shopping trolley and she said, 'I'm all right duck. Just delivering me papers.')

But right now, I don't feel good. I feel enraged. He stands in front of me and asks again patiently, 'Don't you think it's all rather self-indulgent?'

And because he is questioning something which has been my rock and my salvation and rescued me from countless episodes where I have simply not known where to go, I am unable to answer. I am unable to plant my size 4 Converse trainers firmly on the floor and come up with something reasonable and appropriate.

He says, confidently, that he's known who he was since he was twelve and never wasted time navel-gazing and dwelling on the past. We need to focus on the future, he says. The past is gone. Let's all be useful.

My husband, with years of handling people tucked firmly under his belt, carefully, and at great length explains to him why we run this course on spiritual writing. He says with some authority that in his experience, many people do not know themselves and need help to guide them to some degree of self-awareness. They need confidence to discover who they are and what they are good at. It's a journey and we are all on it. Writing is a wonderful way to go back and talk to your younger self who maybe didn't have the tools then to process the negative inputs around at the time. It's a fantastic way to spill out on the page, raging, 'GOD, I HATE YOU!' It's a safe way to ask all those difficult questions, 'WHY ME, LORD?' It's a holding place to weep copious tears onto the page, knowing that it will go no further unless you choose it to.

It's between you and God and God, being God and all, can take it. And then, being the writer that you are, you can go back and craft it if you want to. Hone it. Sharpen it. Polish it. You control it instead of it controlling you.

And, you know what? You are one step away from the immediacy of those emotions and you are able to work with them. You talk about them rather than from them. And this gives you freedom, freedom to express yourself without alienating any reader who might just be a tad alarmed by your murderous or suicidal intentions.

But the Reverend isn't convinced. I venture to enquire why he signed up and he tells me that he had to complete his number of training days for his diocesan ticky-box appraisal and he could make this Thursday. We sign off his attendance and he catches the bus home.

And that's okay. Free speech, individuality and all that.

But this is the thing you see. Writing can be dangerous. Subversive even. It can take you to places you didn't know were there and you won't find out until you take that first step. So it takes a teeny-weeny bit of courage – but only the courage to start. Courage is honed by practice and the more you write, the more your courage grows. A bit like Winnie-the-Pooh's Eeyore mumbling, 'You never know till you try.' And you have to want to do it and even be a little

Writing as therapy

bit hungry for it because then the words write themselves and can take you to glorious places, places of self-discovery, of realisation, of recognition. And then moments of luminosity, of transcendence, when you know you have been touched by God.

And it might come as a surprise to you – but trust me – you don't have to be in line for the Booker prize to use writing as a therapeutic tool. Anyone can do it. And whilst all the pesky little commas and full stops and baffling sentence construction rules you snoozed through back in the days of 4A are useful and necessary at times – you don't need to worry about them here. No one is marking your work or even reading it (unless you want them to).

There's no right or wrong way to use writing as a therapeutic tool. (To be honest, I can get quite antsy when I'm told 'there's no right or wrong way' when I want to learn something and am minded to retort tetchily, 'How do you do it then?') But honestly – there's no right or wrong way.

Because what we're talking about here is using writing as a low-cost, easily-accessible form of self-therapy. We are discussing 'therapeutic' writing not therapy as a medical intervention. Therapy as a medical intervention is of course highly effective, but not everyone has the need, means or inclination for it.

I was a bit, shall we say, hacked off the other week when a nascent writer I know shared with me that another, published writer had told her that 'she wasn't really a writer' because she didn't want to be published. I nearly choked on my Fairtrade decaff. Because I just don't believe that and also feel, shall we say, less than happy with that particular message being fed to people who are struggling with writerly confidence anyway. We are all writers. If we want to be.

I always knew I loved to write. It gave me a sense of self, of accomplishment, of achievement. It was something I was good at. Writing was encouraged in my house because it was seen as a valid tool of encouragement for the committed as well as a weapon with which to preach

The Art of Spiritual Writing

the gospel. From a very young age, I patiently tapped out inspiring words of salvation on my dad's old Olympia typewriter and sent them off to be published in the Young Folks section of the *Redemption Tidings* which plopped onto our doormat faithfully each week. In the absence of anything 'worldly 'in our house such as the *Beano* or, later, heaven forbid, *Jackie* with its references to subversive ideas such as boys and lipstick, I devoured 'Uncle Tom's' page for children in this worthy journal. He regularly exhorted us to, 'BRING THEM IN!' and invite three little chums to Sunday School. Ever one to encourage the fledgling missionaries, he asked them to send him a letter saying how they got on with their evangelistic endeavours. He was sure the small unsaved would be 'thrilled' to be asked to Sunday School. I didn't share his conviction as my vast experience in the playground taught me that most kids were bemused and derisory of my message of the Last Days.

Now there are a number of memoirs out there detailing the realities of growing up in a Christian fundamentalist household. People like Jeanette Winterson, Tara Westover and Jodie Chapman have written powerfully and movingly about their experiences of being brought up with their church's version of the 'Truth'. (Details in Signposts at the end of this book if you want to take a look.) And one thread running through all these recollections is how the faith they were fed was based on fear. Fear of God, fear of hell, fear of people outside the fold. Churches which on the surface looked full of acceptance and love but were anything but.

So, okay, I know some people who grew up in these kinds of churches and have stayed there. It's the way they choose to worship. And that's just fine. Each to their own. I guess I am learning to live and let live with this and not discount or criticise simply because my views don't align with theirs. The Early Church Father Tertullian, in the second century remarked, 'See how they love one another' of Christians and we could maybe take a tip from him on this one.

Writing as therapy

But constantly terrified of getting God wrong, I grew up, painfully anxious, I worried. Endlessly. All the time. About everything. School, homework, getting into trouble, The Rapture, Russia invading, the nuclear threat, my health, Armageddon, boys, bullies, not reading the Bible enough, not praying properly so not being saved … the list went on and on. I could never get to the end of it. And as with the noble army of scribblers before me, I marched to the tune of the pen and the paper and said what I thought.

But when I was doing this, there was nothing to show me the way. Feelings weren't talked about so much back in the day, and certainly not in our house. You put up, shut up and trusted in the Lord. And anyone who admitted to mental health issues at school or in the workplace was at best met with concerned incomprehension. At worst, with sniggers and oblique references to men in little white coats coming to take you away.

I would have loved a book which gave me permission to talk and name all the questions, doubts and difficulties, hurts and longings which cracked off inside me and which I didn't know what to do with. I would have loved ideas on how to talk to God and say what I was feeling. I would have loved a book on therapeutic writing. But I didn't have one.

Although people have been writing ever since Sumerian farmers used reeds on clay to create contracts 3,500 years ago, it wasn't until the late 1980s that the term 'expressive writing' began to be used by the American, James W. Pennebaker. He encouraged participants to, 'Write your very deepest thoughts and feelings about the most traumatic experience of your entire life or an extremely important emotional issue that has affected you and your life. In your writing, I'd like you to really let go and explore your deepest emotions and thoughts.'

Since then, there has been a proliferation of books and methods on how to use writing as a therapeutic tool and, trust me, there's really no one-size-fits-all approach. It's all about finding your own voice. I can't say that enough so I'll say it again. It's all about finding your own voice!' And here are some tried and tested routes which others have found helpful. A 'how to do it' section if you like. Have a go.

Writing letters

Writing letters seems a bit old hat now, doesn't it? The eye-watering cost of a stamp makes the whole process seem very last century. But some still like to make the thoughts in their head turn into squiggly marks with pen onto paper. I must say, I get a real thrill if a real envelope addressed to me in real handwriting plops onto the doormat. Mostly today though, people use email and it's the same process really. It's making the thoughts in your head appear on a screen rather than on paper. So whichever way suits you best – think about writing a letter if there's something you really want to get off your chest to someone. That someone could be God, or it could be someone else – a friend or a family member or your boss. It could even be to a hurt or injured part of yourself. Tell them how you feel. You don't have to post it or click 'Send'. It's enough to write it.

Write your story

There are two ways to do this. You can either start at the beginning and go straight through or pick a particular memory and write about that. Here is a memory of mine, aged four, of the opening of my nascent fundamentalist church. It really helped me to write this.

> The church was a little wooden hut set on a patch of scrubland in a cul-de-sac on the edge of the council estate built with much sweat and tears by the men of the fellowship. It seemed a long way to walk to church because my dad had once told me that our road was as long as Jonah's whale and I knew that was the biggest living thing in the Bible, so it followed that our road was the longest

Writing as therapy

anywhere too. I was a compliant child who never questioned the assertions of the adults around me that the Bible was the literal truth of God. So it was a tiring prospect to walk up the back of Jonah's whale to church three times every Sunday. Being chosen had its drawbacks.

It was an awesome day in 1968 when it was finally opened for God's business and we all watched as Miss Baxter, a doughty Church Army veteran was accorded the immense privilege of cutting the ribbon with an opening prayer. She was dressed in her Sunday best which must have had her sweating on this August day, woollen stockings, a long sombre threadbare grey winter coat, no-nonsense lace-up black boots and her felt hat jammed firmly on her head. Not a glimpse of flesh to be seen lest it tempt the unwary to lustful thoughts. Though Miss Baxter was hardly a pin-up girl for the swinging sixties. Her claim to notoriety which certainly impressed me when I was a child was that the famous missionary, Gladys Aylward, had once spent a night at her house.

I am four years old at this event and hanging uncertainly on the edge of our nascent Sunday School who have all turned up to sing 'I am H-A-P-P-Y' as loudly as they can to impress the visiting brothers and sisters. Never a child to be confident around strangers, I have my thumb, as ever stuck firmly in my mouth as emotional back-up in this worrying landscape. As befitting the enormity of the occasion, I am wearing my best outfit of a dress with a flared skirt and one of my Auntie Lily's chunky knitted cardigans. I know today is important and I need to behave as befits the daughter of the Heavenly King.

Around the honoured guest cluster the group of pilgrims who have made this happen.

The Art of Spiritual Writing

Chiefly my parents. My dad stands ill at ease in his shiny suit, hands in pockets, face set in a tense grimace, clutching his black Bible. He has an impossible task ahead of him. He is only thirty-five and responsible for saving his neighbours, providing them with all their spiritual sustenance as well as turning up six days a week to a grim job he hates. No wonder he looks stressed. Next to him is my mum. She has been called, she says, by the Lord to save at least five souls a day and brims with the hope of filling this place every week. Other more seasoned pastors edge this group having brought their congregations to swell the ranks and encourage our little band of disciples.

The doors are ceremoniously swung open and everyone troops in. It's a small space inside so some of the faithful are left outside and have to peer through the windows and the open doors. Inside, it is freshly painted and decorated with flowers for the ceremony. Decorations are unusual and not encouraged since the exhortation to not make any graven image is central to the tenets of the faith, but flowers are permitted on this day. Serried ranks of chairs, donated by a local Baptist church, a snip at £5 (they were upgrading) fill the central space. There is a small platform at the far end (no truck here with east and west and such Popery) with a plain lectern on it for the pastor's Bible, and an embroidered banner proclaiming in purple lettering, 'JESUS CHRIST IS LORD.' There are no crosses and certainly no statues. Oliver Cromwell may have been the first Puritan but he set a benchmark for austerity which fundamentalist churches have aspired to ever since.

Glance to your right and there is a cast-

Writing as therapy

iron stove with a chimney reaching up and out of the roof. On this first summer day, it stands idle but in the bitter winters to come, it is much pressed into service. My dad would heave great shovelfuls of coke into its gaping maw as he stoked it up, ready for the Sunday morning congregation to make their chilly way through the streets to sing praises and warm themselves by the twin fires of God's love and my dad's coal. I spent many long meetings (we didn't call them services) rubbing my small frozen hands and warming my bare chilly legs around that source of heat. Other children had similar ideas and Christian forbearance was decidedly absent as we pushed and jostled and pinched each other out of the way, all the while lustily singing, 'Rescue the perishing.' It was sheer bad luck if you needed a wee in these Arctic conditions as the toilets were built on the outside and you would have to brave the snow drifts and unheated lavatories or risk wetting your pants in the meeting, which would never do.

So there I am, four years old, sandwiched between my two grandmothers watching my parents on the platform, my dad preaching the Word of God, my mum sitting next to him in her rightful supporting role as a woman. I believe everything I see and hear. I am already convinced of my exclusion from the fold because I know deep deep down where the sun doesn't shine that I will never make the grade. Something inside me locks and bolts leaving me firmly on the outside.

Faith is a journey. This is the beginning. And it is many many years before I began to undo the locks and bolts and discover a different God.

Don't worry about your memory being entirely accurate. It might not be. What you will be writing is how it was for you, how you experienced this situation, the effect it had on you. Write about others if you want to (top tip: stop short of Actual Libel if you are going to publish). But don't hold back otherwise. As my very favourite writing mentor Anne Lamott says, 'You own everything that happened to you. Tell your stories. If people wanted you to write warmly about them, they should have behaved better.'

Write a list
Not in the mood for writing? Just write a list. Here are some examples to try,

- Things I find difficult to understand

- Things that irritate, frustrate, or deaden me

- Things that excite me or bring me to life.

To be honest, if your list says fish fingers, bin bags, bananas, you probably really aren't in the mood for writing and maybe you need to have a nice little nap. Or write about your memories of fish fingers. Just saying ...

Or you can write your feelings
Pick a feeling and write about it. How are you feeling right now? Write it. Or you can recall a feeling rather than having one right now. Anger? Joy? Jealousy?

Here is a piece of my writing on anger which found hugely therapeutic to write. In this piece, I am writing **about** my anger rather than **from** it. Doing this helped me turn my anger into prayer. (By the way, I also write frequently in my journal from my anger. 'I HATE YOU! WHY DID YOU SPEAK TO ME LIKE THAT!!!') I haven't included that writing here as it might scare the horses. You can do it though.

Writing as therapy

Much against my better judgement, I took myself off to the January sales last week. My jeans were, shall we say, rather tight after the Christmas festivities and much as I told myself that they'd shrunk in the wash, I needed something elasticated and comfortable like they have in the back of 'Woman's Weekly'. I'd like to think of myself as the sort of person who would much rather be running through a field of wheat or shinning up a mountain than trying clothes on, but the boring truth is, I like a good sale. I like the thrill of the chase, the fingering of the fabric, the 50% OFF! ticket, the glow of pure satisfaction when it fits. Call me shallow if you like. I do.

Anyway, hunt over, kill made, I set off back to the car park only to be arrested by the sight of a bloke preaching on the street corner. This was my experience as a kid, standing with our merry little band, handing out tracts and exhorting passers-by to be saved and so I felt some natural affinity with him. It was not a warm day and hats off to him, he was standing up there and doing it.

But his billboard depressed me. No – I'm being too nice to myself. It enraged me. I wanted to eyeball him and screech, 'YOU CANNOT BE SERIOUS!' It made me want to turn to the assembled little throng hanging on his every word and shout, 'RUN FOR YOUR LIVES!'

I did none of those things. I must say, I am fairly house-trained these days in the niceties of spiritual debate. In fact, I didn't say anything. I didn't want to start an argument in the middle of the city centre with someone who may or may not be into listening and responding appropriately.

So I walked away and prayed for him instead and for all the people around him. I can't type that without a glow of amazement and satisfaction – even though it doesn't quite square with trying to be humble. I managed to turn around my homicidal rage into prayer and I thank God and my companions on the journey for that.

I did take a sneaky pic of his billboard on my phone though to show my husband when I got home, and just, you know, talk through if you like. I like doing this and my ever patient and accommodating other half doesn't mind. The preacher's billboard said,

There are only two kinds of people.
Unsaved. Lost. Guilty. Condemned.
Or Saved. Redeemed. Forgiven. Justified.

He was handing out his own helpful little tracts telling me how to be in the Saved and Redeemed camp but I could have told him chapter and verse, growing up as I did in daily terror that I hadn't done it properly and would forever be Unsaved. Lost. Guilty. Condemned.

And call me old-fashioned but I just won't buy it anymore. I don't buy a God who would damn most of his creation because they haven't read that tract. And I am astounded by grace. The grace of God which enables me to talk about that manic anger, that gives me the resources to reach into myself and pray for the source of my fury instead of letting it fester and gnaw away inside me doing all sorts of damage. As it could have done and certainly would, once upon a time.

I'm learning what to do with the roaring volcano inside. Otherwise known as pain.

Writing as therapy

Now you don't have to look for painful memories to write about. Honestly. You don't have to dig deep and find moments which ring your earliest bells and which you would rather not enable to see the light of day. It's not for everyone. We can all have feelings here and now which are equally as valid and powerful and resonant.

How do you feel about what's going on right now in your street, your community, your village, town or city, your country, your world? What are your passions? Climate change? Wars and rumours of wars? Inequalities all around us? Those fleeing their homeland to reach a place of safety? Those who feel abandoned, left behind, ignored?

Write about them. Ask God to embrace us, comfort us, restore us in all this bedlam. God reads what we write.

What to do with your therapy writing – four ideas

You could do nothing with it. You've written it – or as I feel sometimes – it's written you. It's done its job. You have made the inside come outside and it hopefully it feels better. You have brought your-self into the light. You have found your voice. You have given yourself permission to name the nameless, feel the feelings, ask for what you need. You can control it instead of it controlling you. Job done.

Or you could share it with someone. Maybe someone you trust. It's sometimes a helpful way of sharing your feelings, but at a bit of a distance. Many times in my conversations with my priest-friend, I would hurl a piece of writing at her as I left the room, knowing full well I wouldn't have to talk about it until the next time we met. And not even then if I didn't want to. You will know who you want to trust with your-self. It may be a friend, a member of your family, a priest, therapist. You can even read it to the dog if you like.

You may want to redraft it. I often redraft pieces as that's when I find the nuggets of gold in them. It's when I begin to make sense of what I have written and find myself writing myself into an answer. Or if not an answer, something of an understanding. I do not however redraft my journal. That's sufficient for the day.

Or you may just want to keep going. If you have found it helpful to write like this – keep going! Trust me, it will begin to have an effect on your life. You will be able to know yourself better, understand what is happening, work things out. Write about that difficult relationship that's messing with your life at the moment. Write about the bully in the playground who's now wanting to be friends on Facebook. Write it all down and hold it firmly in its place.

Writing prompts

Here are some sentence prompts to get you going. Perhaps you don't know what to write, but you know you need to write. Try one of these ...

- I am most happy when ...

- When I was little, I saw ...

- I have trouble sleeping when ...

- I am worried about ...

- I find joy in ...

- I was so angry when ...

There are a lot of writing prompts given throughout this chapter. You don't have to do them all (unless you want to). Maybe pick one, one that appeals to you and just begs for your attention.

And if you are finding it difficult to process anything that arises in your writing and feel some help is needed, there is some guidance in Signposts.

CHAPTER 8
Writing as prayer

My writing is simply praying on paper.
Anon, participant on one of our Spiritual Writing retreats

I (Eirene) love watching my little toddler grandchildren work things out. Maybe that block won't fit in that hole. Maybe the baked beans are touching the chips. Maybe you peel the banana all the way down, when they wanted to do it themselves, and ruin their lives. Or it's time to go back in the car seat and there's no way they are ready. And their natural and healthy reaction is to scream. This is sometimes quite hard on the adults around them, but having successfully navigated this stage of development themselves, they are able to take a deep breath, summon reservoirs of patience, and help the little red-faced, incandescent bundle of frustration ride out the storm. It's called being an adult.

Sometimes my prayers feel like this. Like God is the sensible adult on hand with wet wipes and tissues and drinks and snacks when things get too much. And I really need to talk to God and know I'm being heard. I sit on his knee, hiccupping with misery and need to howl into his shoulder until the storm passes. I guess that's prayer. But sometimes I just need a big hug and a calm chat. And writing as prayer can do both of those things for me.

I make a distinction between writing *a* prayer and writing *as* prayer. Maybe writing *a* prayer is an intentional prayer. You sit down with your quill or your pen or your

The Art of Spiritual Writing

laptop and craft a prayer which can be prayed, not only by you but by others around you. Maybe even generations to come, although you might not know that at the time. And writing *as* prayer is perhaps when you are not consciously constructing a prayer, but your writing becomes that. It may not be intentionally a prayer, but someone else – maybe hundreds of years hence will use it like that.

The distinction doesn't really matter as long as the prayers are there and they lift and sustain and draw us closer. The connection is through the words rather than how they were put together. So writing can be prayer – intentional or unintentional. Every letter and word I put on the page can be prayer. If I want it to be. Everything I say and write is communication with God or Love or whatever name there is which doesn't terrorise or alienate. Writing as in reaching in and taking hold. Being connected. Life.

And, Julia Cameron says, 'Although we seldom talk about it in these terms, writing is a means of prayer. It connects us to the invisible world. It gives us a gate or conduit for the other world to talk to us whether we call it the subconscious, the unconscious, the superconscious, the imagination, or the Muse. Writing gives us a place to welcome more than the rational. It opens the door to inspiration. It opens the door to God...'

It's all about connection. Everything that matters is about connection. When I feel abandoned, I am frightened and tense and miserable and lonely and watchful and mistrustful and angry and not my-self. But when I am connected to someone or something, I am able to breathe. I am able to flourish and relax and smile and be happy and say – 'This is me!' And I am okay. So when I write – I am connecting to God. I am saying 'God. This is me. I want to be connected.'

What would God write back? What would she want to say to me? She would tell me that she is reliable. She is loving. She is consistent. She is accepting. She is not

Writing as prayer

judgemental. She is warm. She loves me. And this God would not demand that I follow a straight and narrow path and use God-language to communicate in prescribed ways. This God asks nothing of me but that I am truly and authentically myself. And helps me to be my best self. Not in any pious or righteous way – but in the way that means I am truly set on solid ground and I am happy. That is the God who I invite to speak to me in writing. That is the God I write to. And who writes back.

Now I haven't always experienced my writing as prayer. It came as something of a revelation to me a few years ago that every word on the page could be a breath connecting me to God. That writing could be a medium whereby I could talk to God and God could talk back. Here's how it happened ...

> I'm in the middle of a coast-to coast walk. And before I hear any murmurs of congratulation, appreciation, admiration, or wonder, you need to know something. I haven't pulled on my walking boots, donned my cagoule, purchased a pole, and set off with my trusty Wainwright for company and a map of all the potential watering holes between St Bees in Cumbria and Robin Hood's Bay. No. My coast-to-coast challenge is, shall we say, internal. It's a spiritual coast-to-coast. And before anyone ventures to say it's not the same – it's not. It's much harder.
>
> When you begin a journey, sometimes you can only see your next step. And that's if you're lucky. You may have no idea about the bigger picture. Maybe your walking companion does, but this information needs to be drip fed in small doses. Otherwise, the reality may be too overwhelming. And it's only by looking back that you can see how far you have come and realise

that you are not the same person who set out at the beginning.

Things have changed. I have changed. But I'm not there yet.

The shoreline behind me has long since receded and I have lost sight of the sea. And there is a vast swathe of countryside between me and the next shoreline way into the distance. I don't know exactly what's there. But I have survived all kinds of tests and trials, much as Frodo Baggins in *The Lord of the Rings* with his allies and travelling companions did when they took on the Dark Lord Sauron and the forces of darkness to win back their treasure. Not that I'm any Tolkien, or even a courageous and fearless hobbit you understand. I'm on a journey facing storms, high winds, torrential rain, hail, snow, fire, floods, and enemies who may harm me. That's about as far as the analogy goes. And there may be more of all that to come and I don't know, but I've touched hell already and I'm still here to tell the tale.

Sometimes I wonder if there could be a shorter route. Say the eight miles from Penzance to St Ives which I could cover in two and a half hours rather than the hundred and ninety miles of the northern route which takes at least fifteen days. But I know there isn't. Not for me anyhow. Some people tackle the shorter route and it's what they need. There's no right or wrong about this. You choose the coast-to-coast that's right for you and for what you need to do.

On my walk, I've had to let go of the messages in my head. The ones that tell me to believe in a God who will punish me if I don't get it right. Send packing the God who frightens little children and tells them they will be banished from the Kingdom if they are not brimming with joy unspeakable

> and full of glory. I am discovering another God – the one from *The Shack* who wipes her floury hands on her apron as she bakes an apple pie and makes me sit down at the table and eat. A Mother God who watches over me tenderly while I sleep and is there when I wake. But, however much I want that God in my head, the other one still insinuates itself, snake-like into my psyche, whispering over and over that I am lost. For now.
>
> But this god is losing its grip, because as you can see, these are not just thoughts. I am writing them down so that they become a physical presence in black and white on the paper. I sit down at my keyboard and write my story, punching out the words on the keyboard, jaw clenched, teeth gritted, weepily chasing the words across the page. And some of the fragmented shards inside begin to meld together and I know that somewhere, somehow, I am being healed. And it feels a bit like coming home.
>
> Writing can do this. I just have to turn on the tap and let the water flow. Trust my-self to the words and the words will be waiting to be found. Trust my-self to the God who is receiving these words and knows that it's my way of connecting. Of praying.
>
> I can write a lot in a hundred and ninety miles.

Just take a moment to think about how you might want to use writing as prayer. What works for you? Where do you find your voice? Turn on the tap and see what comes. Start writing with your pen or your laptop and talk to God.

Intentional and unintentional prayers

Now we are going to consider some of the ways in which writing has been used as writing *as* prayer, intentionally or unintentionally over hundreds of years. These are ideas for you to try. Call it a pick 'n' mix. Choose the ways which work for you and jettison those that don't. Remember – you are finding your own voice. Here are four ideas: ancient prayers, hymns as prayer, poetry as prayer and using the Bible to pray.

Ancient prayers

Imagine early scribes, hunched over their parchment, scribbling in a dank garret by the light of a flickering candle (bit of poetic licence here). They would not have imagined for a second that their words would be read and savoured in the second millennium. I think they would have been much more concerned with how their words impacted on the people around them and in communicating their message for their time. (And not getting their heads chopped off for being a Christian or for being the wrong sort of Christian.) Yet the fact that their writings still enable others to reach out and connect with God for themselves, shows them to be intensely powerful prayers. Here is one unknown author from the fifteenth century:

> God be in my head, and in my understanding;
> God be in my eyes, and in my looking;
> God be in my mouth, and in my speaking;
> God be in my heart, and in my thinking;
> God be at my end, and at my departing.

This was originally written in French with the first English version found in a Book of Hours printed by Robert Pynson in London in 1514. It then found its way into a Sarum Primer of 1558. And now it's one of the most well-known and used prayers in the English language. I remember when I was at grammar school, we used to sing it in assembly every Friday. Maybe the mistresses thought that a hall full of seven hundred pubescent girls needed a timely reminder of their moral duties before they hit the Locarno on Saturday night. I doubt the French author scribbling away in 1490 could

Writing as prayer

have imagined schoolgirls six hundred years hence would be intoning his words with varying degrees of sincerity and piety.

> 'Thou hast made us for thyself, O Lord, and our heart is restless until it finds its rest in thee.'

This is the opening of St Augustine's *Confessions* which is considered to be the first autobiography written in the Western world. It is an account of St Augustine's early life and youthful indiscretions leading eventually to his conversion to Christianity. St Augustine wrote these books for an audience – and presumably to lead people to conversion just as he had been led, but again I doubt he considered his words would still be prayed almost a thousand years later.

Here is another example of familiar phrases which were penned centuries ago. These are often used as part of the communion service and were written by St Richard of Chichester in the thirteenth century. They have withstood the test of time to become for us, much loved and sustaining words.

> O most merciful redeemer, friend, and brother,
> may I know you more clearly, love you more dearly,
> and follow you more nearly, day by day. Amen.

Try writing your own prayer. It could be a prayer just for you or it could be a prayer to share with others. Or you could try both. Don't worry about using fancy language or having complicated thoughts. Just use your own voice. It may be prayed in 2123. You never know!

Hymns as prayer

One of my very favourite hymns is 'Just as I am' written by Charlotte Elliott in 1835. I just had to write about it.

The Art of Spiritual Writing

The other night, it being All Souls and all, I sang a Requiem Eucharist for the Faithful Departed in my cathedral church. My childhood church didn't keep this particular day in any special way – it just denounced any commemoration of the dead as nasty Popish frippery. But to mark this day, my choir sang Duruflé's Requiem which is a truly gut-wrenching piece of music designed to transport you to the heavenlies along with all those faithful departed (and the unfaithful as well in my view.) But I digress. This piece of music has a lot of twiddly bits in it and so I spent most of the previous week hunched over my laptop, practising my second soprano part with Kings College, Cambridge just to make sure I got all of the twiddly bits right. Kings always does, but to be fair, they do have a bit more time to practise.

I stood there in the service and I felt so utterly and completely and peacefully right at home that it almost hurt. And when we were invited to light a candle to remember loved ones, I lit one for my first husband, Pete, a lovely and gentle priest who died very young. I say I'm not annoyed with God about that now, but if I'm honest, there are times when I do feel a little, shall we say, resentful, as I cuddle the grandchildren he never met. But I loved the chance for him to have his own light flickering there, dispelling the darkness, a shining reminder that death is not the end.

So, all this is happening for me right now and it acts as such a good counter balance to the perpetual record playing in my head that I'm just not good enough. Who the heck do I think I am dressing up in fancy robes to sing, and then compounding my wickedness by praying for the dead? I can just imagine hands being laid on

Writing as prayer

me in the little wooden church of my childhood with muttered prayers for healing regarding my consorting with Duruflé and his like.

But in the end, it wasn't Duruflé who brought me to my emotional knees. Sorry, pal and all that, but while I think your music is astonishing, I was generally concentrating too hard on getting most of the right notes in the right order to have much energy left for feeling. No – it was the final hymn, 'Just as I am without one plea,' which was my undoing, although you will be pleased to hear that I managed not to break down and weep over my white surplice, but stand there and sing and feel all at the same time.

I just love that hymn. It says what I want to say but it makes every word count and even makes them rhyme. I looked it up on Wikipedia when I got home and discovered that the author, Charlotte Elliott, 'lay upon her sofa in her pleasant boudoir' (as you do), and recalling her turbulent sleep the night before when she had felt so utterly useless, questioning the 'reality of her whole spiritual life', penned the words of this hymn. Some girl. Raised in a Christian home (as so many of us were) she felt chronic turbulent doubts and conflicts (as so many of us do) and in writing this hymn helped herself to give them a voice. Then by sharing it with the world, millions of other people could give their fears a name, including yours truly.

So, this is where I go when I feel, shall we say insecure about my place in God's kingdom. Yes – I am 'poor, wretched, blind', and I need 'sight, riches, healing of the mind' (and then some!), but God's love has 'broken every barrier down', and I can come. Hip hip hooray!!

I'll go forward in my explorations singing this hymn and every time it pops up on the service

> sheet at church, I'll know they are playing my tune. And if I feel a little pathetic waste of space in my spiritual life – I will recline on my bed in my imaginary boudoir with a large cup of tea and recite every verse. I am still feeling my way and uncertain of the right direction at times. But I know that because I am loved, I will be shown what I have to do, where my energy must go, where to focus my prayers, my longings, my-self.
>
> As 'Just as I am' says at the end of every verse,
>
> 'O Lamb of God, I come.'

Now I doubt that Charlotte, penning these words in 1835 thought that they would have such a profound impact on a cathedral chorister in 2023. But she wrote them down and saved them and shared them and they were kept and savoured and treasured and sung by millions.

What are your favourite hymns? What words move you? Choose a hymn and find out about it. Realise the connection between the person who wrote those words however many years ago – and you – experiencing them now. Maybe write down your response to the hymn. Find your voice and say how it feels for you.

Poetry as prayer

Some may argue that all poetry is prayer, coming as it can do, from the guts, from that place deep inside where the sun doesn't shine. The place where all aspects of the human condition are found. Love. Joy. Grief. Hope. Despair. I once heard of poetry described as the ability to say as much as possible in as few words as possible. (Clearly Edwin Atherstone didn't get the memo when he wrote 'Israel in Egypt' in 1861 at 20,000 lines). But some poetry, addressed directly to God is sublime prayer. Here is an example. This is 'Come my Way' by George Herbert.

Writing as prayer

Come, my Way, my Truth, my Life:
such a way as gives us breath;
such a truth as ends all strife;
such a life as killeth death.

Come, my Light, my Feast, my Strength:
such a light as shows a feast;
such a feast as mends in length;
such a strength as makes a guest.

Come, my Joy, my Love, my Heart:
such a joy as none can move:
such a love as none can part;
such a heart as joys in love.

Some may know this as a hymn as John Wesley got his hands on it in 1739 and adopted it for his *Hymns and Sacred Poems*. And then Vaughn Williams set it to music in 1911 for his *Five Mystical Songs*. But it was first and foremost a poem.

Do you have a poem you pray with? Here are some ideas. If you want to, you can research it and understand more about what was going through the writer's mind as they wrote the words. Or just choose one and pray it. Or pray a favourite from your treasure chest.

- I never saw a moor   Emily Dickinson
- Tune me, O Lord   Christina Rossetti
- Suddenly   R. S. Thomas
- The Journey   Mary Oliver
- I saw him standing   Ann Griffiths trans. Rowan Williams
- Love   George Herbert

The Art of Spiritual Writing

Praying the Bible

Now there are almost 728,000 words in the NIV version of the Bible and a few hundred more in the King James (but to be fair, they did have a few more thys and thous to get in). Some may say that the whole of the Bible can be a prayer, but I would struggle with that – what with Numbers 7 and its account of the offerings for the tabernacle in precise detail times twelve. Or Genesis 5 with its family tree from Adam to Noah including ages. It's interesting that Noah fathered Shem, Ham, and Japheth when he was 500 years old (and we thought Bernie Ecclestone was going some at 89) but to be honest, I couldn't pray with a list of names. Maybe you could – remember this is all about your journey.

A good example of praying with the Bible are the Psalms which are a glorious collection of poems, many of which are addressed directly to God. In my book that counts as prayer.

Praying with the Psalms

I was thinking about some of my very favourite verses from the Psalms which I would use as prayer. 'Be still, and know that I am God' (Psalm 46:10) is definitely one. I would pray this when I'm having a day when 'all my tabs are open' as I frequently say to my husband. A day when I can't switch off and am in hyper micro-managing mode.

Another is 'You, Lord, are forgiving and good, abounding in love to all who call to you.' (Psalm 86:5). Yep. I would pray this when I feel but a worm and have no health in me (Thanks, Cranmer.) And accompanying it would be, 'Because you are my help, I sing in the shadow of your wings' (Psalm 63:7). I would pray this when I'm doing my hair in the morning and singing along to Alexa. I love the thought of being snuggled up all cosy and warm in the shadow and shelter of God's wings.

What are your favourite verses in the Psalms? Can you use them as prayers?

Reflections and meditations

Some of us may like to write reflections and meditations, either for our own prayer, or to help others to pray. Let's have a look at this form of writing, especially the difference between the two. Jessica Mehring sums this up very well, 'In reflection, the purpose is to engage the mind. Unlike meditation, where the purpose is to turn off or dim our thoughts, in reflection we activate our thinking. We actively contemplate something – a goal, challenge, situation, decision or simply some information we've consumed.'

Dr April McIntyre, an experienced published writer of reflections, from our own Derby Cathedral Cafe Writers group has this to say: 'What is the purpose of a reflection? A reflection should be uplifting, moving, challenging or comforting, helping people connect with God and building bridges between life and faith. It should not be evangelistic or contain detailed Bible or academic analysis.' That is spot on.

Writing a reflection

You know when you're sitting in church and the preacher ascends the pulpit or positions their notes on the lectern and you sit up a little straighter and intend to fully listen for however long it takes? And then five minutes later, you're wondering whether to try that recipe for pear and apple crumble, ruminating on the latest twist in EastEnders and worrying about that last phone call with one of your kids? No? Just me then.

I'm far less likely to do that if the sermon begins with a good hook. A bit of a meaty story to draw me in. I like to be involved. Call me shallow if you like. But it's an indisputable truth that we like a good story. And if the sermon, or talk or preach or whatever you call it begins with one, I'm much more likely to hang on in in there.

It's the same with writing a reflection. And like a sermon, it needs a beginning, a middle and an end so the congregation have a chance of keeping up with you and

The Art of Spiritual Writing

it needs to be short and lean (as the best sermons are I think). Unlike a sermon, it's best if it makes just one point so you don't overload your dear reader. Here's one I made earlier:

> A kind of awakening
>
> I like to think of spring as a kind of awakening. I'm not much of a gardener myself, but even I can see little buds beginning to protrude from branches and crocuses poking their heads above the ground and saying 'hello' to the world. It's as if God turns on some celestial switch which alerts nature to the fact that winter, with its dark nights and cold days, is behind us and we can look forward to warmth and sunshine.
>
> Faith can be a bit like that. I grew up in a Christian household but can't honestly say that I felt much of a relationship with the Creator of the Universe, or God, or my Higher Power – or whatever name you use, until I was about twelve. At that point, I moved into my local parish church and joined the choir, singing, in true Anglican tradition, the Te Deum, the Jubilate, Venite, Benedicite, Magnificat and Nunc Dimittis, week in, week out. These texts became as familiar to me as my school timetable and my teachers' names. They settled themselves comfortably into my psyche.
>
> Then, imperceptibly, unbidden, the words began to come alive for me and dance. The name of Jesus sent a small thrill down my spine. I couldn't talk about this. The ladies of the choir certainly would have been slightly alarmed at any such revelations and the vicar was a remote figure who'd never seen in anything but a black wool suit and a white dog collar so big it looked like a dinner plate encircling his neck. Anyway,

> he might wonder where I had been with God all this time and I couldn't admit that I'd never really struck up much of a conversation.
>
> Yet, like a gardener in the springtime, I nurtured this little shoot of connection and kept watch over it through years and years of its flowering. Sometimes the weather was really rough and it would retreat for a while, to keep itself safe from being battered by storms. Other times, it would flourish and raise its head high and bask in the glorious light. But it grew steadily and constantly, reaching for the sun.
>
> Faith can be like that. It doesn't have to be a revelation of a single moment in time. If the seed is planted, then just trust that it will grow. God, the gentle and wise gardener, will do the rest.

What is a meditation?

Meditations tend to be longer than reflections and may cover a number of points. (For example – we wrote a series of meditations for BRF where we were given the constraint of 4000 words for a 12-day period.) They can still be based upon your own experiences but may reference the scriptures more fully. Ideas may come from your own prayer – or your own writing as prayer. There will be nuggets in there which you can mine as the seeds of meditative pieces. Think about all the ways in this book which cover writing meditatively – journalling, morning pages, daily writing, writing as therapy and as prayer, freewriting. It can all be grist to the mill for a meditative piece. Just sit with it and let it write itself.

Don't get too hung up on the difference between reflective and meditative writing. It's really not a test. As we keep saying, don't censor or review. Just let it flow. These are meant to be hints and tips – not a straitjacket. You're meant to be picnicking by a bubbling stream on a summer's day or striding across the wild and windy moors – not looking through the bars of a prison cell.

So, there are a few tips and observations on writing as prayer, reflections and meditations. Any writing which comes from the heart is a prayer. For years, I would beat myself up for being hopeless at prayer. But I wrote. And I think that God was listening to my words on the page just as much as if I'd said them out loud. Please don't separate your writing and your prayer. They are one and the same. You are one glorious whole in your creativity and your yearning to connect with your Creator.

Writing prompts

Writing a Psalm
As writers, we could try writing our own psalm (aka prayer). Here are three ideas to get you started...

Write your own psalm of lament: sadness
Read Psalm 42 and then think about what has this week been like for you? How are you feeling right now? Can you identify the emotions which have been around for you – maybe just under the surface or very much present in your everyday life? What are these feelings? All feelings are valid – even so-called negative ones. Have you felt worried? Anxious? Depressed? Sad? Impatient? Frustrated? Have you felt that at times events are out of your control?

As you prepare to put pen to paper, close your eyes and imagine God is sitting right next to you. He/she can hold your hand if you like. Now tell God everything – all about what it's like for you, all those feelings, all your pain. God will not judge or condemn so feel absolutely safe to say anything.

Writing as prayer

Now try writing.

First of all, say 'Hello' to God. Make your complaint direct to him.

Tell God about the problem you are grappling with. Tell her the details.

Tell God that you trust him. Tell her that you know he can help.

Say 'Thank you' and praise God for his/her constant faithfulness.

Write your own psalm of thanksgiving

Recognise the good things in your life. Have a conversation with God now and tell him/her how grateful you are. Praise God for all he/she has done and is doing for you.

Write your version or transliteration of a psalm which has special meaning for you.

For example, Psalm 124. This was my prayer after a very tough time:

If you hadn't been with me Lord
when I was overwhelmed
I would have gone under the waves
disappeared without a trace.
I was almost swept away by the tide
And would not have survived.
I almost drowned,
swallowed by the icy water.

I want to praise you Lord
For protecting me.
For rescuing and restoring me.
For sustaining and supporting me.
For setting me down on the dry land.
I ask you for help
My Good God.

The Art of Spiritual Writing

It can be as long or short as you like – Psalm 117 has two verses and Psalm 119 has 176. Go for it.

CHAPTER 9
The marvellous metaphor

The quality of your language is significant. In your dark night, try speaking in story and images. Resist the attempt to explain, defend and interpret. Use metaphors and symbols.

Thomas Moore, *Dark Nights of the Soul*

And finally, we'd like to bring in our friends, metaphors! We love them. I (Richard) am one of their greatest fans and if they were a football team, I'd buy their home shirt every season. But what exactly are they? The Concise Oxford English Dictionary defines them as 'A figure of speech in which a word or phrase is applied to something to which it is not literally applicable. A thing regarded as symbolic of something else.' To sum up, it is something representing something else.

Adding richness

One of the limitations of writing is that it is visually unappetising. It is black on white. We talked earlier about journalling and the benefit of using graphics and illustrations to enliven and enhance our writing. Giving the reader a picture to look at helps to lift the written word. In this chapter we look at ways to give the reader a picture through the words we use, adding colour to the words by using metaphors and other figures of speech.

The Art of Spiritual Writing

Metaphor is a long standing and integral part of the human experience. It is commonplace in all cultures and particularly richly represented in religious teaching and texts. Its power is in its imagery and ease of remembering. The oral tradition was historically the way in which the leaders of a tribe, family or culture would pass down the rules of living and lessons in life. And metaphor has always been a useful means to do this.

From the creation stories, such as Genesis, through the life of Christ, the Bible is a story rich in parable and symbolism. From Aesop's fables, fairy stories, nursery rhymes and a host of other stories, we find metaphor and imagery around every corner (that's a metaphor, incidentally).

To take a well-known example, consider the parable Jesus told of the farmer sowing his seed. The seed was a metaphor the word of God.

'A farmer went out to sow his seed. As he was scattering the seed, some fell along the path; it was trampled on, and the birds of the air ate it up. Some fell on rock, and when it came up, the plants withered because they had no moisture. Other seed fell among thorns, which grew up with it and choked the plants. Still other seed fell on good soil. It came up and yielded a crop, a hundred times more than was sown.' This translation of Luke (Luke 8:5-8 NIV) tells the metaphorical story in 84 words. Possibly one of the world's best known and most eloquent metaphors. It is a prime example of a metaphor telling the story for all to understand.

Other parables of Jesus speak powerfully through story. For example, the foolish builder who builds his house on sand. The mustard seed which grows exponentially large from such a small, planted seed. The good Samaritan, who tends the needs of the roadside victim whilst two supposedly worthy people ignore his needs and pass by. The lost sheep talks of the shepherd who leaves the 99 other sheep to go and find the lost one. These are simple stories that portray very clearly a much deeper truth.

The marvellous metaphor

Metaphor and imagery bring words to life. They turn the black and white into colour. They hold the reader's attention, and add a depth of flavour to your writing. If you think of your writing as a casserole, these are the herbs and spices, *the magic secret ingredients,* as the TV chefs call them, that add something special.

Metaphors and more – imagery and idiom

Some will say the above metaphor of the sowing of the seeds is not a metaphor but a parable. Others will say it is an extended metaphor. It matters not for the purposes of this discussion. We use all sorts of methods as writers to add imagery to our stories.

The Simile

A close cousin of the metaphor is the simile. A simile includes the word *as* or *like*. I used it above, when suggesting you to think of your writing *as* a casserole. There are thousands of examples of which you will be aware. Here's a few common ones to illustrate the point – swim *like* a fish, as hard *as* nails, eat *like* a horse, white *as* a sheet. The English language is rich in the use of simile.

The use of idiom

And we can also conjure up imagery through the use of idiom. Idioms are not literal description but we draw conclusions from their imagery. Here are some common ones: He gets up my nose. She's pulling your leg. It's water under the bridge. Keep your powder dry. To put all your eggs in one basket.

Anyone interested in idioms will find a treasure trove of these in *The Dictionary of English Idioms, from Cloud Nine to Seventh Heaven,* published by Penguin Reference and there are many other books listing such figures of speech. See Signposts for further information.

You can, of course, create your own metaphors and idioms, which will create more traction with the reader.

They do not need to be profound or detailed. For example, the idea of our writing being like a casserole is an original metaphor that I used to convey the idea of adding flavour to writing to enhance its impact.

Using metaphor to tell a story

Writing does not need to be factual when you tell a story. If you are a reporter for a newspaper or writing instruction manuals and the like, of course it needs to be straight factual information. With spiritual writing, this is far less the case. It is by its very nature a great place to use the writing tools mentioned above. For example, when narrating a part of your spiritual journey, it is perfectly acceptable to use such methods as metaphor or other imagery. In fact, there may be parts of your journey where the straightforward telling of the story may lack the colour you would like to portray and a metaphorical slant may be helpful. For purposes of illustration, here is an example from my own writing of the use of metaphor to capture some of the essence of a part of my own journey.

In 2008, I started a year's course in personal coaching. In retrospect, it was the best programme I've ever completed. It was a tough start as we were deliberately thrown in at the deep end with no models or reference points. Just get on with it, they said. The initial modus operandi was to learn from your mistakes and triumphs. I wrote a learning journal throughout the programme and included a metaphor at the start of this journal, entitled *The Field*. It rabbited on a bit so I won't reproduce it here. But essentially, it said this:

At the start of the course, I felt I was totally lost and disorientated, walking uphill in a large field in heavy mist, almost fearful. I could see no boundaries, no fences or hedges to guide me. There were no outlines to give me reference points. I felt totally alone. But I sensed that time would burn off the mist and I'd gradually see clearly what the whole subject was about. As we progressed and learnt

The marvellous metaphor

so much so quickly, I began to see where I was, and where we were heading. I was getting my bearings. The metaphor continued that I would eventually see the whole field and then the whole valley that was the world of coaching. After that, one day I might walk off and discover other valleys and perhaps even discover new things to share with others about coaching. That was the general content of the original metaphor.

And three years later, looking back the metaphor was correct and somewhat prophetic. The next valley turned out to be my training as a spiritual accompanier, another very different form of 'coaching'. I could then bring the experiences of both of those valleys together. This metaphor really helped me through the year's course as I gradually progressed from unconscious incompetence to a competent practitioner and the landscape cleared before me. It carried me forward in my learning journal and helped me to avoid becoming overwhelmed by unknowing.

I share this story with you because fast forward 12 years and I was writing a piece on metaphors for another course I was undertaking. One night, I went to bed mulling the subject over in my mind and reflecting on my old story of *The Field*. The next morning, I awoke at 6 a.m. with the following story coursing through my mind. It was part two of *The Field*. What had started as a metaphor for my coaching course transitioned into a metaphor for what was happening now in both my writing and spiritual journey. And it insisted that I got out of bed and write it straightaway. Spiritual writing sometimes does that to you. It emerges from the deep, bites you on the bum, and demands to be recorded. If this happens, get up and write before it fades away. The metaphor continued thus and this time included people. For some reason, I am the observer of this later instalment and I wrote the story from the second person point of view.

The Art of Spiritual Writing

... But then, after so long you realise there are still new terrains to explore. And you carry on through this marvellously symbolic countryside and go down lanes, over hills, climb mountains, and get stuck up blind alleys, clambering over metaphors the whole time. And you realise after a time that your original metaphor was sadly lacking. There were no people in it. And you need people because the road is getting tough and they are an integral part and key component of any spiritual journey and are central in the recent part of your journey.

So, the story is upgraded as the journey continues. Along a hot sunny road, you come to a lone bistro in the middle of nowhere and you enter. There is a wonderful woman standing behind the well-stocked counter. There are no other customers. You start to talk to her and she grasps everything that you are saying. She brings you food and drink to a table outside and a pack of supplies for the rest of your journey. The food is delicious. You sit and talk for ages and her eyes smile at you the whole time You realise that you can do nothing but love her. And when you finally set off on your way, her presence won't leave you alone.

You walk for a solitary day and the next morning he appears. He was bound to turn up sooner or later and sure enough round the next corner, he is waiting for you in the middle of the road, tall and stout with a full grey beard, a long staff, flowing robes. Oh, no. So stereotypical. Your heart sinks but he explains there's tough ground ahead and he's going to help you over the mountain pass. You soon find that your image of him is wrong. You've misunderstood him and start

The marvellous metaphor

to grow closer to him. He transforms from bumbling strict father to loving guide. He understands your needs. He protects you through the cold nights, leads you safely over the slippery ice-bound ledges and narrow trails. You now want him with you and trust him implicitly.

And, in time, your journey starts to drop down over the other side of the mountain range to a softer, warmer countryside and you notice the wonderful green gently-hilled landscape. It is awesome and you turn around to thank him but you can no longer see him. He has vanished from sight. But somehow, he is still with you.

After some time, a fork joins the road from the right and another angel appears. Here is a young man, tightly-curled hair, fit, with a tanned face, casually dressed with a leather belt around his waist carrying a small satchel on his side. He asks if he can walk with you and introduces himself as the Storyteller. He has no belongings other than the small leather bag on his belt. We walk. I ask of the bag. He says it is all he needs for his journey. It is his scriptorium and contains all the stories ever told. I look quizzical and he touches it.

He becomes more animated, in voice and body. Excited and engaged, he starts to tell me many stories. He points out the small spring bubbling up from the rocks we pass. We follow its course downhill. Joined by other streams we note how it grows to a babbling brook. Onwards it goes. He traces its path with his finger pointing into the distance, as it plunges over the waterfall, into a deep calm pool. Then on further, thickening and aging its way seawards. You can't see yet where it meets the great sea of everything, he says, but one day you will see and understand its joining and transformation.

The Art of Spiritual Writing

The river knows the journey of life, he whispers.

He shows me a garden full of so many plants. He talks of sowing seeds and the pollination they need, the weeds and the care and maintenance. He describes how they all need the right conditions to grow. Dry soil or damp shade. Like us, they can only thrive if placed in the right conditions at the right time. And don't forget to prune, he says. Always cut back. It promotes new growth. He asks if I've heard the parable of the sower. I nod.

The garden changes to forest. His arms wave extolling the beauty of the stout high trees, the ancient yews, inter-tangled roots sucking their life from the soil, sharing their resources and talking with one another. They reach so high, producing fruit and shade. He's excited how they protect and feed one another and shed their fruit and seed. They are a sacred model of our lives. So many metaphors. The landscape is crazy with models.

Out of the woods, we come to an animal park, where he indicates the creatures. There are snakes in the grass, rogue elephants, stubborn mules, leopards that cannot change their spots. He sees I am scared and says not to worry. They cannot hurt us because he can change the story at any time. But these are some of the things you might meet, he suggests, laughing hyenas, crocodile tears, kangaroo courts and frogs looking for throats, a whole idiomatic menagerie, teeming with the symbolism of the animal kingdom. My head is buzzing with symbols and allegories and similes as we stop for the night and share the supplies from my bistro lady.

In the morning, he says he must leave. He asks me to remember that this is my journey, but there many other different types of journeys. He regales me with examples of other sorts of journeys – tales

The marvellous metaphor

of island hopping, railway journeys of special stations visited and carriages full of the people, stormy sea voyages, comfortable world cruises, route marches, and space travel to imaginary worlds. And don't forget the circumnavigation, he says, coming back to where you started. T. S. Eliot reminded us of that one in his *Four Quartets*, he tells me.

He touches his bag and his stories stop. I think you have sufficient metaphors to last you for a long time, he smiles. He waves me goodbye and turns off the road. 'I've other stories to share today. I must be gone,' he tells me. 'But I will come again to see you one day. Here is your new valley lying before you. This is the valley where you must write the story of the spiritual journey and share it with many so that they can tell their stories.' He walks calmly away, leaving me with so many ideas.

You walk down to your newly-discovered valley. It is so clean and fresh and unexplored. And in the first small town of honey-coloured stone cottages, you are drawn towards a larger building in the square, built in the same local stone. The door is open and beckons you inside to an exquisite library, such a peaceful and inviting place. You sit down amongst the books, enchanted. And you know, you just know, here is every book you have ever read and every book you will ever need. This is your own private scriptorium. There are racks and racks of special books, unique to you. You pick one out.

It is called *Childhood* and as you open it, it bursts into Disneyesque rapture, with video footage, music, sensations, smells and people from your early days. You are so excited that you choose another. This is called *Mentors*. It's full of stories of all who have smoothed your life's path for you. On the last page are your recent trio – the lady from the bistro, the Storyteller and the guy with the grey beard. And then a book called *Bedrooms*, full of clips of your childhood rooms of safety and comfort and private space, progressing on to boudoirs of love and the X-rated material we made together, for our eyes only.

There are books on every subject you need. You note some – *The University Years, Career, Grandparents, Grandchildren, When God Came Round to Tea.* This is you. And you see the large bookcase that is marked *Emotions*. It has so many books – *Fears and Worries, Betrayed, Answered Prayers. Intuition, Forgiveness Given and Forgiveness Received.* You note the *Forgiveness Received* is a lot thicker than its sister volume. And there is a Dictionary entitled *Every Word You Know.* You riffle through some pages and it is correct. You know all the words. You don't have to leave the table. These books come to you at will.

You then realise there are no books on the future. From here you must forge your own story. And the library is abuzz with your stories that can help. There are lots of reference books of *Hopes and Dreams, Doors to Push* and *Planting Seeds.* And there are books on *Pruning, Talk with Friends, Daydreams, Discernment* and *Scriptures.* You recognise that you are now fully in Metaphorland.

You go and find a hostelry. They don't have bars in Metaphorland, only hostelries, because it is a place of poetry. You know this, because the Storyteller told you so. The land reminds you of Betjeman's Metroland, a special created space of specially-created things. And you want to sit down and write a poem about it. You are thirsty and order beer from the lady behind the bar. How fitting. She is your lady from the bistro who

The marvellous metaphor

> smiles knowingly at you. And you go to your table and take out your notebook. You are so tired from your journey. You haven't the energy to write this poem. It then dawns upon you. You have already written it down just here right now, and you have captured the essence of what you have found in Metaphorland. And you can relax. This *is* the poem.
>
> You sense someone behind you, then feel her reassuring hand upon your shoulder, the closeness of her body and the warmth of her breath. You drink deeply, conscious that you will be together joyfully tonight and always. And God is in his heaven and the Storyteller's blessings are yours.
>
> And tomorrow, you must rise, go shopping, mow the lawns, and the man is coming to fix the boiler. For you can settle now. You have arrived in this sacred space, where you can reflect and write your stories of the spiritual journey to share with others, so that they, too, may write theirs. And you want to do it so much. Because it is the best story you ever heard and you want to tell it. And you will.

So that was my metaphorical story and one that still speaks so loudly to me of my spiritual journey. It is sketchy, allegorical and metaphorical, but it says so much to me personally and for me is so much more powerful than a factual recitation could ever be.

Some ideas for developing metaphors

There follow a few ideas on how to develop your own metaphors. As with all writing, don't be afraid to kick your idea off and see where it takes you. Anne Lamott observes the following in *Bird by Bird* – 'The garden is one of the two *great metaphors for humanity. The other, of course, is the river. Metaphors are a great language tool because they explain the unknown in terms of the known.'* These are undoubtedly two of the best metaphors and both appear in the example of my own personal metaphor above. But here are other good fields to explore for good metaphors.

The journey

I also added the journey as a metaphor in my example. Some find it useful to think of their journey as metaphor. What sort of journey was it? It may have been a magical mystery tour when you are unaware of your destination for which you are heading, or a well-planned and executed voyage. It could be like a hitch-hiking holiday where you need people to help you to get from A to B. Or was it a fast and comfortable ride down the motorway, a difficult trek across hard terrain, a railway journey with many others on board and several changes, or a treacherous sea voyage? The likelihood is that it will be a mix of many of these but there may be a sort of journey that best describes your own spiritual walk at this particular time. Look for a journey metaphor that best suits you. In chapter nine, Eirene describes her journey using the metaphor of a coast-to-coast walk.

Animals

Animals are a rich source of imagery. They provide a fascinating and diverse range of possibilities to symbolise people and situations. Below is a random list I drew up to spark ideas

dodo	rabbit	lion
mole	eel	walrus
swan	goat	greyhound
snake	sparrow	spider
robin	salmon	giraffe
shark	duck	kangaroo

The marvellous metaphor

beaver	chameleon	cat
reindeer	rat	owl
lizard	butterfly	fox
honey-bee	locust	flea
dinosaur	crab	turkey
lamb	goldfish	wasp
tiger	crocodile	ostrich
carthorse	whale	turtle
hippo	ferret	elephant
chicken	frog	terrier
worm	monkey	mosquito

Note that each of these animals conjures up a unique and powerful image. The dodo is extinct, the carthorse hardworking, the reindeer suggests Christmas, the wasp is irate, the butterfly gracious. And many have given their names to figures of speech. Scanning the list, I quickly thought of the following – to breed like rabbits, ferret out, chameleon-like, meek as a lamb, sticks her head in the sand like an ostrich, beavering about, worming his way.

Nature

And there is the whole of nature to call upon. My personal metaphor used the geographical surroundings a lot to paint the picture. The tree is a great natural metaphor too, the growth from seed to mightiness, the root system feeding up into the myriad of branches where the fruit is produced, another powerful metaphor for life. This can be a good one to draw. In essence, anything in nature is a likely contender for a metaphor. Nature and the Universe are the physical spaces in which we all dwell and hence provide in their richness many symbols with which we are all commonly acquainted. And as a key component of nature, the weather is also a powerful source of metaphor and is often used in films to denote the forthcoming storm or the quieter peaceful times of sunshine.

The House
And finally, the house of many rooms. The house or home provides lots of imagery to consider. You can think of yourself as a house. The things you keep in the attic, the mysteries and ghosts in the cellar, the heart of the home in the warmth of the kitchen, the relaxation of life in the sitting room. Imagine the rooms you have the keys to, locked doors. Think where your house is sited and what is visible from the window. And the garage and garden shed are separate but connected. There is much metaphorical material here.

Try them on for size
There are thousands of ideas in the areas discussed above. Have a go at using imagery, metaphor, simile, idioms and other figures of speech and see how you get on using these writing devices.

> If the random animal list above appeals to you, we'd recommend the *Concise Oxford Thesaurus*. In addition to being a comprehensive thesaurus, my edition has a central section called Wordfinder, which consists of substantial lists on a wide range of subjects from animals to fabrics, music to phobias, shapes to transport and much, much more in between, an interesting sourcebook of ideas when looking for imagery and language.
>
> Scanning my copy, I learn that a phobia of churches is known as 'ecclesiophobia' and the collective name for ducks is a 'paddling' when on water and a 'safe', when on land. Who knew?

The premise herein is that these techniques can add depth and sparkle to your writing. Are there certain ideas here that appeal to you? Do you think that these are or could become a part of your authentic voice? You may find they are not your cup of tea (whoops!). Or you may fall in love with them. Our advice when writing is 'Don't forget to take your metaphors with you.'

Writing prompts

A metaphor of the house
Take a home past or present. Write about one or several of the following elements that you recall from that house.

Sounds and smells. Capture those you associate with the house and surroundings.

Treasures and trivia. Recall what you prized and what had no value to you in the home. Are there keepsakes you have that trigger thoughts for you?

Guests and ghosts. Who were the people who visited regularly? Were there family ghosts that you sensed?

Heartbeat and rhythm. Identify the beat of the house, the rhythm of life there and the effect it had upon you, morning, noon, night, weekdays, weekends.

My favourite room
In a page and a half of A4, write about your favourite room. Describe it physically or write what feelings and emotions it triggers in you.

Pick a metaphor
Were there any of the metaphors that appealed to you? Some major areas discussed are the garden, the river, the journey, the tree, animals, the weather, nature, the Universe. Pick a favourite or develop one of your own metaphors and apply it to something that is bubbling away in your mind.

CHAPTER 10
And finally ...

After nourishment, shelter and companionship, stories are the thing we need most in the world.
Philip Pullman

We all have stories. We may love our stories and want to tell them. We may try to forget. But we all have stories and they make us who we are. And in this book, we have looked at ways to bring our stories out into the light and enable them to be told. We may tell them to other people or only to ourselves and that is absolutely fine. But the telling will bring release and relief, hope and healing as we discover our authentic voice and share it, maybe for the very first time.

But remember, writing is a journey. We've talked a lot within this book about the diverse nature of our own individual spiritual journeys and how that can inform and encourage us to write. And as we suggested at the very beginning, you can also think of your reading of this book as an individual journey. There is a host of ideas and suggestions you could pursue. Our guess is that no two readers will take the same path in exploring their writing. Your forthcoming writing journey is, in essence, a metaphorical mirror of a personal spiritual journey. Hence our individual writing journeys will vary substantially.

So, our advice is to be prepared to pick your own favoured pathway through the material in the book and go with what feels good for you. If you feel lost, go back

And finally ...

and try another path that may have passed by. No writing is ever lost. All is of value and worthwhile and what feels like today's writing misadventure may lead you to new insights and fresh horizons.

However, there is one constant. Like any skill, writing improves with practice and as your journey continues, your knowledge and skill will grow. If you wish to take your writing further after you have read and digested this book, there are ample suggestions and further reading ideas in Signposts, the final chapter.

Some things you will have to consider are where you write – either in your home or elsewhere. And the time of writing. A fixed time to write can help if that works for you and you are able to do it, but likewise some are more haphazard and write when the Muse strikes. One common theme that emerges in most books on writing is that the morning seems to be the favourite writing time. But don't make lots of rules. We both prefer writing in the morning, but unusually I'm writing this final chapter in the evening.

There is a smorgasbord of ideas about freeing up your writing – journalling, freewriting, daily pages, writing as prayer, writing as therapy, metaphor. All are valid ways to explore your writing as they grant you permission to be free, to write freely about any subject to any length (remember Eirene's green exercise book) and can help you to discern your next steps, your preferred genres and your style.

And look at ways to fill the well with new ideas and improve creativity by observing more closely the world and people. Also try new stimulating activities. Read more widely. It will improve your vocabulary and the style of your writing. I (Richard) know for certain that when I am reading a lot, my writing is far more fluent. And a notebook?

Finally, please don't be alone. Like all art, writing is a personal activity, but getting together with others who also write can be so encouraging and enriching. Think about joining a group, find a writing buddy and locate someone

The Art of Spiritual Writing

who will give you honest and valuable feedback (not your Mum).

And never be afraid to start. A blank page with no ideas can seem hopeless. Just start putting some words down. They are magic. They will invite you in, make you welcome, ask you to carry on, encourage you to dance and lead you into another world.

Don't do all this at once. It will drive you crazy and you'll have to give up the day job. But we hope that you have found at least three to four good ideas that appeal to you immediately to take with you as you set off on your voyage of discovery. Note them. Give them a try. If certain chapters stick in your mind – read them again. If you like a particular exercise – write it again.

No musts, but all considerations to ponder on your writing journey.

And oops, yes, spiritual writing! It might be a good idea to pray for your writing, whatever prayer looks like to you – traditional, a time of meditation, a moment of silent contemplation.

We are firm believers that writing is a gift and as a God-given gift, we should develop it and share it with others. So don't be afraid to step out.

This book is all about helping you to find your authentic voice. And maybe discovering a bit more about yourself on the way. And maybe a bit more about God as well. Rumi said, 'I searched for God and found only myself. I searched for myself and found only God.' He must have written that down.

Someone once said that 'all stories need telling'. That is so true. We have included some short family stories that were recorded in writing long ago, but have found their way into this book where they will be read by many more (we hope!). You never know where your writing will end up. All stories need telling. Find your authentic voice and tell yours. The world will thank you.

And remember – what you write is enough. You are

And finally …

enough. Our belief is that God is a God of grace. She is always there, with arms wide open, waiting for you to run into them and be sheltered just like a mother hen shelters her chicks. (Psalm 91 since you're asking.)

And telling you that you are okay, because you are. And telling you that your individual story needs telling.

Be who you are. And write.

Go well.

CHAPTER 11
Signposts

If you want to be a writer, you must do two things above all others: read a lot and write a lot. There's no way around these two things that I'm aware of, no shortcut.

Stephen King

Here is a list of resources to assist you on writing journey.

BOOKS

There are many good general books about writing. We can't list them all. But all of the books in this chapter have been read by us and come with our personal recommendation.

The following three are, in our opinion, the best general introductions to creativity and writing and are recommended texts for those interested in spiritual writing. We recommend *Bird by Bird* by Anne Lamott as the best general introduction to creative writing. *Writing down the Bones* by Natalie Goldberg is also full of wonderful advice. And *The Artist's Way* by Julia Cameron is superb if you are looking for something to improve your creativity and also includes her Morning Pages and Artist's Date tools, invaluable for writers.

There are lots of books on creative writing but we have recommended these three writers as they come the closest, in our opinion, to the values of spiritual writing. It is certainly worth reading at least one of these if you are serious about improving your writing skills.

The following recommendations will lead you to more specific interests in writing and are likely to appeal as you develop specific interests on your writing journey.

Creative writing coursebooks
Get Started in Creative Writing, Stephen May (Teach Yourself series)

The Creative Writing Coursebook, Julia Bell and Paul Magrs (eds.) (University of East Anglia)

Creative Writing, Linda Anderson and Derek Neale (Open University)

First You Write a Sentence, Joe Moran

Creativity
Mind Mapping, Tony Buzan

The Mind Map Book, Tony Buzan

The Creative Act, A Way Of Being, Rick Rubin

Journalling
Keeping A Spiritual Journal, Edward England (ed.)

The Creative Journal, The Art of Finding Yourself, Lucia Capacchione

Spiritual Journalling: Recording Your Journey, Richard Peace

How to Make a Journal of Your Life, D. Price

Memoir (how to write memoir)
The Accidental Memoir, Eve Makis and Anthony Cropper

Writing Life Stories, Bill Roorbach

The Art of Spiritual Writing

Memoir (other people's memoir)
I Know Why the Caged Bird Sings, Maya Angelou

Holy Smoke, Libby Purves

Rosie: Scenes From A Vanished Life, Rose Tremain,

Educated, Tara Westover

Oranges Are Not The Only Fruit, Jeanette Winterson

Why Be Happy When You Could be Normal?, Jeanette Winterson

Oh, Sister, Jodie Chapman

Obituaries
Lives Less Ordinary: Obituaries of the Eccentric, Unique and Undefinable, Nigel Farndale (ed.)

The Very Best of the Daily Telegraph Books of Obituaries, Hugh Massingberd (ed.)

Poetry
Poetry in the Making, Ted Hughes

How to Write Poetry and Get it Published, Matthew Sweeney and John Harley Williams (Teach Yourself series)

The Ode Less Travelled: A Guide to Writing Poetry, Stephen Fry

Psalms
Psalms for Praying, Nan C. Merrill

Reading for writers
Reading Like a Writer, Francine Prose

The Art of Fiction, David Lodge

Spiritual journey
God of Surprises, Gerard W. Hughes

Landmarks: An Ignatian Journey, Margaret Silf

Signposts

The God You Already Know, Henry Morgan and Roy Gregory

Writing the Sacred Journey, Elizabeth Andrew

Sleeping With Bread, Dennis, Sheila and Matthew Linn

In Search of a Way: Two Journeys of Spiritual Discovery, Gerard W. Hughes

Style, grammar, and punctuation
Have You Eaten Grandma? Gyles Brandreth

Eats, Shoots and Leaves, Lynne Truss

Word reference
Concise Oxford Dictionary

Concise Oxford Thesaurus

Dictionary of English Idioms, From Cloud Nine to Seventh Heaven, Daphne Gullard and David Hinds-Howell

Oxford Dictionary of Modern English Slang, John Ayto and John Simpson

Writers on writing
On Writing, Stephen King

A Moveable Feast, Ernest Hemingway

Becoming a Writer, Dorothea Brande (version with the foreword by Malcolm Bradbury)

The Writing Life, Annie Dillard

Writing as prayer
Conversations with God, Neale Donald Walsh

Writing comedy
The Serious Guide to Joke Writing, Sally Holloway

Comedy Writing Secrets, Mark Shatz and Mel Helitzer

The Art of Spiritual Writing

Writing fiction
The Art of Fiction, David Lodge

Writing Short Stories, Ailsa Cox

Writing a Novel, Nigel Watts, Teach Yourself series

Writing as therapy
The Writer's Key: Introducing Creative Solutions for Life, Gillie Bolton

The Creative Journal: The Art of Finding Yourself, Lucia Capacchione

Writing habit
Daily Rituals, Mason Curry

Daily Rituals: Women at Work, Mason Curry

Rooms of Their Own: Where Great Writers Write, Alex Johnson, James Oses (illustrations)

Essays
There are many books of essays by wonderful writers which are inherently spiritual in nature as they talk about what it is to be human, faith, the life journey and everything else in between.

Blue Nights, Joan Didion

Almost Everything, Anne Lamott

Travelling Mercies, Anne Lamott

This Sunrise of Wonder, Michael Mayne

What We Talk About When We Talk About Faith, P. Stanford (ed.)

The Faraway Nearby, Rebecca Solnit

Signposts

Magazines
Writing Magazine

Writers' Forum

Christian Writer, Association of Christian Writers (ACW)

Together magazine – resourcing Christian retailers, suppliers and writers.

GROUPS

Writers' groups can be invaluable if you want to develop your skills. You can get new ideas and insights from your fellow writers, learn about local writing events and competitions, get feedback from others on your writing and maybe find a writing buddy. Some will have guest speakers. But more than ever, you can find encouragement and support.

Most towns will have a group of some description. If at first you don't succeed, shop around until you find a group that meets your needs. More groups have developed an online presence post-COVID, enabling members to join them from a wider region. This can expand your horizons and some meet internationally.

Looking online is a good way to find local writing groups. Just Google 'writing groups near me' and see what comes up. If you prefer, ask in your local library or community centre. Or ask around if you are a member of another social group such as the WI, church, evening class, book club or such. Someone will have come across one, somewhere. We writers get around! We were very surprised when we set up our own writers' group at how many closet writers came out of the woodwork. And so often, the refrain we heard on those joining our group was 'I'm not a writer but…' And then after a little while, they realised they were.

Writing can be a lonely business, so getting some support, inspiration and encouragement from other writers can be very helpful. A writing community can offer a safe space in which to risk exposure and encouragement wherever you happen to be on your writing journey. Some groups will also offer more 'formal' input at each meeting, such as a guest speaker.

The aim is to go away feeling that you have learned something, forged networks or sparked new ideas.

COURSES AND RETREATS

There are so many. Choose carefully. Personal recommendations from trusted friends are the best way to help you choose the right one for you. Also be sure to check out the leader's credentials.

Two that we come across regularly are courses run by the Arvon Foundation. And the Swanwick Writers' Summer School in Derbyshire, founded in 1948, runs an annual week's retreat.

OTHER IDEAS

Take heed of Stephen King's advice to 'read a lot.' We all tend to stick to favourite authors and tried and tested genres. Try something different. If you are a detective novel fan, try romance, sci-fi or a classical novel. Try new authors. Scan the best seller lists. You can experiment at no cost by joining your local library or by buying cheaply in charity shops, where no doubt, you will find a selection of second-hand nearly-new novels.

Pick up a magazine. These are full of adverts, commentary, letters, specialist articles, new ideas, interesting fillers, letters and so on. Try and read something out of your normal range of interest, as it will spark new ideas and insights. Borrow from friends and observe the magazines in reception areas and libraries.

Signposts

Check out the on-line news website BBC.co.uk. As a general stopping off point for current affairs and trends, this is an invaluable site. It has, of course, all the news but much more – long reads, general interest items, newspaper highlights, short educational videos and so on. There are often links to further information. It is well worth a daily visit to dig around for ideas and for items of current interest.

The internet. Where do you start? Here it is, the portal to all the world's information. And of course, misinformation. But there are lots of sources of creative and new ideas here to peruse and pursue. YouTube is a valuable source of ideas and will provide information on anything from changing a lightbulb to quantum physics and everything in between. It can also remember your browsing history and flag up material in those areas. TED talks are also a good source of new and emerging thinking. And, of course, there is a myriad of information on social media, and in podcasts and blogs where you can follow thought leaders and special interest groups to enhance and stimulate your creativity. Also consider following your favourite writers on their website, blogs, and social media accounts. You can often subscribe to their email circulars as well.

And finally ...

We know that writing about your-self and remembering painful incidents and feelings from your past can be hard. If you are struggling, don't be alone. Talk to someone – a family member, a friend, a work colleague, a confidant, or a minister. And there are always professional counsellors and therapists. You can find one through the British Association for Counselling and Psychotherapy. There is always the ACC too – the Association for Christians in Counselling if you would specifically like a Christian counsellor. And don't forget – if you are really struggling you can ask for an appointment with your GP. Don't battle on alone. There is always help.